Your biscuits will be beautiful every time if you measure ingredients accurately, and use correct-sized eggs. Remember to have those eggs and butter at room temperature. These guidelines and more appear on page 128, with a helpful list of oven temperatures. Then, follow our baking times carefully for scrumptious results.

Pamela Clark
FOOD EDITOR

BRITISH & NORTH AMERICAN READERS: Please note that Australian cup and spoon measurements are metric. A quick conversion guide appears on page 128.

Almond Chocolate Fingers

60g butter
1 cup (125g) packaged
 ground almonds
½ cup (110g) caster sugar
2 eggs, lightly beaten
2 tablespoons plain flour
100g dark chocolate, melted
1 teaspoon vegetable oil

TOPPING
60g butter, chopped
⅓ cup (75g) caster sugar
⅓ cup (80ml) glucose syrup
1½ cups (120g) flaked almonds
2 tablespoons water

Beat butter, almonds and sugar in small bowl with electric mixer until smooth, add eggs, beat until just combined. Stir in sifted flour; spread over base of greased 26cm x 32cm Swiss roll pan. Bake in moderately hot oven about 10 minutes or until lightly browned; cool 5 minutes.

Spread base with topping, bake in moderately hot oven further 10 minutes or until lightly browned. Cut while warm; lift onto wire racks to cool. Dip biscuits into combined chocolate and oil; leave to set on wire racks.

Topping: Combine all ingredients in medium pan, stir over heat, without boiling, until sugar is dissolved. Bring to boil, simmer, uncovered, without stirring, 4 minutes or until thickened slightly.

Almond Raspberry Fingers

125g butter
1 teaspoon grated lemon rind
½ cup (80g) icing sugar mixture
1 cup (150g) plain flour
⅓ cup (80ml) raspberry jam

TOPPING
2 cups (250g) packaged
 ground almonds
2 tablespoons caster sugar
2 eggs, lightly beaten
1½ tablespoons dark rum

Beat butter, rind and icing sugar in a small bowl with electric mixer until smooth, stir in sifted flour. Knead gently on lightly floured surface until smooth. Roll dough between sheets of baking paper to a 23cm square. Place on greased oven tray; prick lightly with a fork. Bake in moderately hot oven about 10 minutes or until lightly browned. Spread gently with jam while hot.

Spoon topping into piping bag fitted with a large fluted tube. Pipe topping in lines over jam, about 1cm apart. Bake in moderate oven about 10 minutes or until lightly browned. Cut while warm. Cool on tray.

Topping: Combine all ingredients in bowl; mix well.

LEFT: Almond Raspberry Fingers.
RIGHT: Almond Chocolate Fingers.

Almond Maraschino Biscuits

Kirsch, or many other types of liqueur, can be substituted for Maraschino, if preferred.

¾ cup (110g) plain flour
¼ cup (30g) packaged ground almonds
¼ cup (55g) caster sugar
60g butter, chopped
1 egg yolk
2 teaspoons Maraschino, approximately
¼ cup (35g) slivered almonds, toasted, chopped

MARASCHINO ICING
1 cup (160g) icing sugar mixture
2 teaspoons Maraschino
2 teaspoons hot water, approximately

Combine sifted flour, ground almonds and sugar in medium bowl, rub in butter. Add egg yolk and enough liqueur to mix to a soft dough. Knead dough gently on lightly floured surface until smooth, cover; refrigerate 30 minutes.

Roll dough between sheets of baking paper until 3mm thick. Cut into 6cm rounds, place about 3cm apart on greased oven trays. Bake in moderate oven about 10 minutes or until lightly browned. Cool on wire racks. Spread biscuits with maraschino icing, sprinkle with slivered almonds.

Maraschino Icing: Sift icing sugar into small heatproof bowl, stir in liqueur and enough water to make a stiff paste. Stir over hot water until spreadable.

Makes about 25.

Almond Slice

A madeira or butter cake is best for the cake crumbs required for this slice.

40g butter
2 tablespoons caster sugar
1 egg yolk
⅔ cup (100g) plain flour
1 tablespoon self-raising flour
200g dark chocolate, melted
2 teaspoons vegetable oil

FILLING
2 eggs, separated
¼ cup (55g) caster sugar
1 tablespoon lemon juice
1 tablespoon honey
60g butter, melted
¾ cup (90g) packaged
   ground almonds
1 cup (100g) plain cake crumbs

TOPPING
125g butter, chopped
½ cup (110g) caster sugar
2 tablespoons cream
1½ cups (120g) flaked almonds
⅓ cup (55g) sultanas,
   coarsely chopped
2 tablespoons coarsely chopped
   glace cherries

Beat butter, sugar and egg yolk in small bowl with electric mixer until smooth. Stir in sifted flours in 2 batches. Press mixture over base of greased 19cm x 29cm rectangular slice pan; spread with filling. Bake in moderately hot oven about 20 minutes or until filling is set and lightly browned. Spread filling with topping; cool. Refrigerate slice until topping is set before cutting.

Dip base and sides of rectangles in combined chocolate and oil; place, chocolate side up, on wire racks until set.

Filling: Beat yolks and sugar in small bowl with electric mixer until thick and creamy. Beat in juice and honey. Stir in butter, almonds and crumbs. Beat egg whites in another small bowl with electric mixer until soft peaks form. Fold egg whites into almond mixture.

Topping: Combine butter and sugar in medium pan, stir over heat, without boiling, until sugar is dissolved. Bring to boil, simmer, uncovered, stirring occasionally, about 5 minutes or until lightly browned. Remove from heat, stir in cream and remaining ingredients.

Apricot Biscuits

Packaged almond or marzipan paste can be used in this recipe.

100g packaged almond paste
90g butter
2 teaspoons grated lemon rind
¼ cup (55g) caster sugar
1 egg, separated
1 cup (150g) plain flour
1 teaspoon water
½ cup (40g) flaked almonds
½ cup (125ml) apricot jam,
**   warmed, sieved**

Beat almond paste, butter, rind, sugar and yolk in small bowl with electric mixer until combined. Stir in sifted flour, knead gently on lightly floured surface until smooth.

Roll dough between sheets of baking paper until 5mm thick. Cut into 5cm rounds, place about 3cm apart on greased oven trays. Brush rounds with combined egg white and water; sprinkle with flaked almonds. Bake in moderate oven about 12 minutes or until lightly browned. Brush biscuits with jam, bake in moderate oven further 5 minutes. Cool on wire racks. Makes about 30.

Apricot Almond Slice

90g butter
¼ cup (55g) raw sugar
1 cup (160g) wholemeal plain flour
2 teaspoons water, approximately
½ cup (40g) flaked almonds

FILLING
1 cup (150g) dried apricots
½ cup (125ml) water

TOPPING
2 egg whites
⅔ cup (150g) raw sugar

Beat butter and sugar in small bowl with electric mixer until smooth. Stir in sifted flour and enough water to mix to a firm dough. Press dough over base of greased 19cm x 29cm rectangular slice pan. Bake in moderate oven 15 minutes, spread with hot filling, then topping and almonds. Bake in moderate oven further 20 minutes or until lightly browned. Cool in pan.

Filling: Combine apricots and water in pan, simmer, covered, about 10 minutes or until apricots are soft and liquid absorbed; blend or process until smooth.

Topping: Beat egg whites in small bowl with electric mixer until soft peaks form. Gradually add sugar; beat on high speed 5 minutes. Sugar should not dissolve.

Apricot Nut Slice

¾ cup (110g) plain flour
¼ cup (35g) self-raising flour
1 tablespoon caster sugar
90g butter
1 egg yolk
⅓ cup (80ml) apricot jam

TOPPING
1 egg white
⅓ cup (75g) caster sugar
2 teaspoons cocoa
⅓ cup (30g) coconut
1¼ cups (185g) unsalted
  roasted peanuts

Sift flours and sugar into medium bowl, rub in butter. Add egg yolk; mix to a firm dough. Press dough over base of greased 19cm x 29cm rectangular slice pan. Bake in moderate oven 10 minutes, gently spread with jam; spread with topping. Bake in moderate oven further 20 minutes or until topping is set. Cool in pan.

Topping: Combine all ingredients in bowl; mix well.

LEFT: Apricot Almond Slice.
ABOVE LEFT: Apricot Biscuits.
ABOVE: Apricot Nut Slice.

Wholemeal Bran Biscuits

2 cups (120g) unprocessed
  wheat bran
1 cup (160g) wholemeal plain flour
2 tablespoons raw sugar
125g butter, chopped
2 eggs, lightly beaten

STEP 3
Press each half of dough over bases of greased 26cm x 32cm Swiss roll pans.

STEP 4
Mark dough into squares; prick with fork. Bake in moderate oven about 15 minutes or until lightly browned. Cut biscuits where marked. Cool on wire racks.

STEP 1
Combine bran, sifted flour and sugar in medium bowl; rub in butter. Add eggs; mix to a soft dough.

STEP 2
Knead dough gently on lightly floured surface until smooth. Divide dough in half.

Bran Butter Biscuits

½ cup (80g) wholemeal plain flour
2 teaspoons baking powder
1 teaspoon raw sugar
½ cup (30g) unprocessed
  wheat bran
60g butter, chopped
2 tablespoons water, approximately
1½ tablespoons unprocessed
  wheat bran, extra

Sift flour and baking powder into medium bowl, stir in sugar and bran; rub in butter. Add enough water to mix to a soft dough. Knead dough gently on lightly floured surface until smooth. Roll dough between sheets of baking paper until 2mm thick. Cut into 5cm rounds. Place biscuits about 3cm apart on greased oven trays; sprinkle with extra bran. Bake in moderate oven about 12 minutes or until lightly browned. Cool on trays.
Makes about 25.

Satay Cheesettes

1 cup (125g) grated tasty
  cheddar cheese
125g butter
1 cup (150g) plain flour
1 tablespoon bottled peanut
  satay sauce
¼ cup (20g) coconut

Beat cheese, butter, sifted flour and
sauce in small bowl with electric
mixer until combined. Roll rounded
teaspoons of mixture into balls; toss
in coconut.

Place balls about 4cm apart on
greased oven trays; flatten with a
fork. Bake in moderate oven about
12 minutes or until lightly browned.
Cool on trays.
Makes about 35.

Bacon Biscuits

2 bacon rashers, finely chopped
60g butter
1 egg yolk
½ cup (60g) grated tasty
  cheddar cheese
⅔ cup (100g) plain flour
½ cup (60g) grated tasty cheddar
  cheese, extra

Add bacon to pan, cook, stirring, until
lightly browned and crisp, drain on
absorbent paper; cool.

Beat butter, yolk, cheese and sifted
flour in small bowl with electric mixer
until mixture comes together, knead
gently on lightly floured surface until
smooth. Roll dough on lightly floured
surface until 3mm thick. Cut into 4cm
rounds. Place rounds about 3cm apart
on greased oven trays; sprinkle with
combined extra cheese and bacon.
Bake in moderately hot oven about
12 minutes or until lightly browned.
Cool on trays.
Makes about 40.

LEFT: Bacon Biscuits.
ABOVE: Satay Cheesettes.
RIGHT: Curry Curlies.

Curry Curlies

250g packet potato crisps
½ cup (40g) coarsely grated
  parmesan cheese
3 sheets ready-rolled puff pastry
150g butter, melted
2 teaspoons curry powder

Blend or process crisps and cheese until finely chopped. Cut pastry into 1cm wide strips. Brush both sides of pastry strips with combined butter and curry powder; press into cheese mixture. Twist strips; place about 3cm apart on greased oven trays. Sprinkle with remaining cheese mixture. Bake in hot oven about 10 minutes or until lightly browned. Cool on trays.
Makes 75.

Cheese Sticks

4 sheets ready-rolled puff pastry
1 egg white, lightly beaten
1½ cups (185g) grated tasty
  cheddar cheese
1 cup (80g) grated parmesan cheese
3 teaspoons paprika

STEP 1
Cut each sheet of pastry into 2cm wide strips; brush with egg white.

STEP 2
Twist 2 strips together to form 1 stick, repeat with remaining pastry. Place sticks about 3cm apart on greased oven trays.

STEP 3
Sprinkle sticks with combined cheeses. Sift paprika over cheese. Bake in hot oven about 15 minutes or until lightly browned. Cool on trays. Makes 28.

Cheddar Cheese Biscuits

1 cup (150g) plain flour
2 tablespoons self-raising flour
¼ teaspoon cayenne pepper
125g butter, chopped
2 tablespoons grated
    parmesan cheese
1 cup (125g) grated tasty
    cheddar cheese
1 tablespoon water, approximately

Sift dry ingredients into medium bowl, rub in butter. Stir in cheeses and enough water to mix to a soft dough. Knead dough gently on lightly floured surface until smooth. Shape dough into a 38cm sausage shape, wrap tightly in foil; refrigerate 1 hour.
  Cut roll into 5mm thick slices, place 3cm apart on greased oven trays. Bake in moderate oven about 20 minutes or until lightly browned. Cool on trays.
Makes about 70.

Indian Curry Biscuits

60g butter
60g packaged cream cheese
1 cup (150g) self-raising flour
1 teaspoon curry powder
pinch cayenne pepper
2 tablespoons milk, approximately
½ cup (60g) grated tasty
   cheddar cheese

Beat butter, cream cheese, sifted flour, curry powder and pepper in small bowl with electric mixer until combined. Stir in enough milk to make ingredients come together to form a firm dough. Knead dough gently on lightly floured surface until smooth. Roll dough until 2mm thick, cut into 5cm rounds. Place biscuits about 3cm apart on greased oven trays; brush with a little extra milk, sprinkle with cheese. Bake in moderate oven about 15 minutes or until lightly browned. Cool on trays. Makes about 40.

Crunchy Cheese Biscuits

125g butter
¾ cup (90g) grated tasty
   cheddar cheese
pinch cayenne pepper
1 cup (150g) self-raising flour
1 cup (80g) crushed Corn Flakes
1 egg, lightly beaten
milk, for brushing

Beat butter, cheese and pepper in small bowl with electric mixer until smooth. Stir in sifted flour, Corn Flakes and egg. Roll rounded teaspoons of mixture into balls, place about 3cm apart on greased oven trays. Flatten biscuits with fork, brush tops with a little milk. Bake in moderate oven about 15 minutes or until lightly browned. Cool on trays. Makes about 45.

LEFT: Indian Curry Biscuits.
RIGHT: Crunchy Cheese Biscuits.

Cherry Almond Bars

90g butter
1 teaspoon grated lemon rind
⅓ cup (75g) caster sugar
1 egg yolk
1 cup (150g) plain flour
⅓ cup (55g) blanched almonds
⅓ cup (70g) glace cherries
250g dark chocolate, melted
2 teaspoons vegetable oil

Beat butter, rind, sugar and yolk in small bowl with electric mixer until smooth. Stir in sifted flour, almonds and cherries. Use floured hands to shape mixture into 4cm x 20cm bar shape; wrap in foil; refrigerate 1 hour or until firm.

Cut bar into 5mm slices, using a serrated knife. Place slices about 3cm apart on baking paper-covered oven trays. Bake in moderate oven about 15 minutes or until lightly browned; cool on trays. Dip half of each biscuit in combined chocolate and oil; leave to set on wire racks.
Makes about 35.

Cherry Nut Biscuits

125g butter
1 teaspoon vanilla essence
¼ cup (55g) caster sugar
1 egg
1 cup (150g) self-raising flour
1¼ cups (185g) crushed nuts
15 glace cherries, halved, approximately

Beat butter, essence, sugar and egg in small bowl with electric mixer until smooth. Stir in sifted flour. Drop rounded teaspoons of mixture into nuts, coat with nuts, roll into balls. Place balls about 4cm apart on greased oven trays, top with cherries. Bake in moderate oven about 15 minutes or until lightly browned. Cool on wire racks.
Makes about 30.

LEFT: Cherry Almond Bars.
RIGHT: Cherry Nut Biscuits.

Funny Faces

60g butter
½ teaspoon vanilla essence
¼ cup (40g) icing sugar mixture
1 egg, separated
½ cup (75g) plain flour
½ cup (75g) self-raising flour
2 teaspoons milk, approximately
assorted sweets

Beat butter, essence, icing sugar and egg yolk in small bowl with electric mixer until smooth. Stir in sifted flours and enough milk to mix to a soft dough. Knead gently on lightly floured surface until smooth, cover; refrigerate 20 minutes.

Roll dough between sheets of baking paper until 3mm thick. Cut into 6cm rounds, place about 3cm apart on greased oven trays. Decorate with assorted sweets and pastry scraps using lightly beaten egg white to attach decorations. Bake in moderate oven about 12 minutes or until lightly browned. Cool on trays.
Makes about 20.

The Big Biscuit

125g butter
1 teaspoon grated orange rind
⅓ cup (75g) raw sugar
⅔ cup (100g) wholemeal
self-raising flour
½ cup (75g) chopped unsalted
roasted peanuts
⅓ cup (55g) sultanas
2 tablespoons orange juice
⅓ cup (30g) coconut
⅓ cup (30g) rolled oats

Beat butter, rind and sugar in small bowl with electric mixer until smooth. Stir in sifted flour and remaining ingredients.

Divide mixture into 6 portions, roll each into a ball. Place balls on greased oven trays, about 10cm apart, flatten with floured hand to about 10cm rounds. Bake in moderate oven about 20 minutes or until lightly browned. Loosen biscuits; cool on trays. Makes 6.

Party Meringues

4 egg whites
1 cup (220g) caster sugar
slivered almonds
assorted sweets

STEP 1

Beat egg whites in small bowl with electric mixer until soft peaks form. Gradually add sugar, beating until dissolved between additions. Spoon a third of mixture into large piping bag fitted with a medium fluted tube. Pipe hedgehogs about 3cm apart on baking paper-covered oven tray.

STEP 2

Spoon half the remaining mixture into large piping bag fitted with a 1.5cm plain tube. Pipe snails about 3cm apart on baking paper-covered oven tray. Spoon remaining mixture into large piping bag fitted with 1cm plain tube. Pipe mice about 3cm apart on baking paper covered oven tray.

STEP 3

Decorate meringues with almonds and assorted sweets. Bake in very slow oven about 45 minutes or until dry and crisp. Cool on trays.
Makes about 36.

Gingerbread People

Gingerbread cutters can be bought at kitchenware shops, or, use the pictures to trace outlines onto firm cardboard. Cut these out to use as guides.
Coloured evaporated milk makes an ideal "paint" for decorating the people.
Use a fine paint brush for best effects.

125g butter
½ cup (100g) firmly packed brown sugar
1 egg yolk
2½ cups (375g) plain flour
1 teaspoon bicarbonate of soda
3 teaspoons ground ginger
½ cup (125ml) golden syrup

ROYAL ICING
1 egg white
1½ cups (240g) pure icing sugar, approximately
food colourings

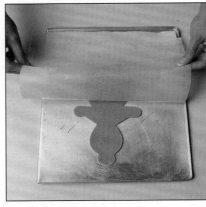

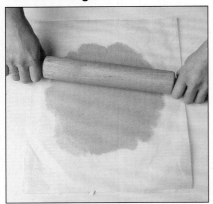

STEP 1
Beat butter, sugar and yolk in small bowl with electric mixer until smooth. Stir in sifted dry ingredients and golden syrup; mix to a soft dough, knead gently on lightly floured surface until smooth. Roll dough between sheets of baking paper until 3mm thick.

STEP 3
Place gingerbread shapes about 3cm apart on greased oven trays. Bake in moderate oven about 10 minutes or until lightly browned. Cool on trays. Spoon icing into piping bag fitted with a small plain tube, decorate shapes as desired.

Royal Icing: Beat egg white in small bowl with electric mixer until frothy, gradually beat in enough sifted icing sugar to give a mixture of piping consistency. Colour as desired. Keep royal icing covered with damp cloth to prevent drying out.

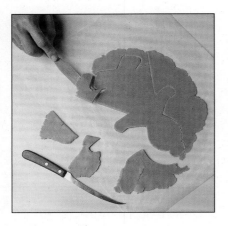

STEP 2
Cut gingerbread shapes from dough.

Chocolate Nut Slice

60g butter
½ teaspoon vanilla essence
1 tablespoon caster sugar
1 egg yolk
¾ cup (110g) plain flour
1 tablespoon cocoa
2 tablespoons chopped unsalted
 roasted peanuts
2 tablespoons coconut
60g dark chocolate, melted

TOPPING
2 eggs
1 cup (200g) firmly packed
 brown sugar
¼ cup (35g) self-raising flour
½ cup (75g) chopped unsalted
 roasted peanuts
1 cup (90g) coconut
1 teaspoon vanilla essence

Beat butter, essence, sugar and yolk in small bowl with electric mixer until smooth. Stir in sifted flour and cocoa. Press mixture over base of greased 19cm x 29cm rectangular slice pan. Spread topping over base; sprinkle with combined nuts and coconut. Bake in moderate oven about 30 minutes or until browned. Cool in pan. Cut into pieces using a serrated knife. Drizzle with chocolate.

Topping: Beat eggs in small bowl with electric mixer until thick, gradually add sugar, beat until combined. Fold in sifted flour, peanuts, coconut and essence.

Chocolate Wheaties

90g butter
½ cup (100g) firmly packed
 brown sugar
1 egg, lightly beaten
¼ cup (20g) coconut
¼ cup (25g) wheatgerm
¾ cup (120g) wholemeal plain flour
½ cup (75g) white self-raising flour
150g dark chocolate, melted
1½ teaspoons vegetable oil

Beat butter and sugar in small bowl with electric mixer until smooth, add egg, beat until combined. Stir in coconut, wheatgerm and sifted flours. Roll rounded teaspoons of mixture into balls, place about 3cm apart on greased oven trays; flatten with a fork. Bake in moderate oven about 12 minutes or until lightly browned. Cool on trays. Dip half of each biscuit in combined chocolate and oil; leave to set on wire racks.
Makes about 35.

ABOVE LEFT: Chocolate Wheaties.
RIGHT: Chocolate Nut Slice.

Chocolate Coconut Bars

125g butter, melted
½ cup (100g) firmly packed
  brown sugar
1 cup (90g) coconut
1 egg, lightly beaten
½ cup (75g) plain flour
⅓ cup (50g) self-raising flour
1 tablespoon cocoa
2 tablespoons coconut, extra

ICING
1 cup (160g) icing sugar mixture
1 tablespoon cocoa
1 teaspoon soft butter
1½ tablespoons milk,
  approximately

Combine butter, sugar, coconut, egg, sifted flours and cocoa in medium bowl; mix well. Press mixture evenly over base of greased 19cm x 29cm rectangular slice pan. Bake in moderate oven about 20 minutes or until firm. Spread hot slice evenly with icing, sprinkle with extra coconut. Cool in pan.

Icing: Sift icing sugar and cocoa into bowl, stir in butter and enough milk to make spreadable.

Lebkuchen

This is our version of an Austrian/German biscuit, traditionally served at Christmas.

60g butter
⅔ cup (160ml) golden syrup
1¾ cups (260g) plain flour
1 teaspoon bicarbonate of soda
½ teaspoon ground ginger
½ teaspoon ground cardamom
½ teaspoon ground cinnamon
½ teaspoon ground cloves
½ teaspoon cocoa
1 tablespoon milk
¼ cup (40g) mixed peel,
  finely chopped
2 tablespoons raspberry jam,
  approximately
185g dark chocolate, melted
2 teaspoons vegetable oil

STEP 1
Combine butter and golden syrup in large pan, stir over heat until butter is melted, bring to boil; remove from heat, stand 10 minutes. Stir in sifted dry ingredients, milk and peel, cover, stand 1½ hours. Knead dough on lightly floured surface until it loses its stickiness.

STEP 2
Roll dough out on floured surface until 8mm thick. Cut into heart shapes about 5cm wide. Place shapes about 3cm apart on greased oven trays.

STEP 3

Make 2cm indentations in centres of shapes, using a floured wooden spoon handle, fill with about ¼ teaspoon of jam. Bake in moderate oven about 10 minutes or until lightly browned. Cool on trays.

STEP 4

Dip bases of biscuits in combined chocolate and oil, smooth off excess. Place biscuits, jam side down on foil-covered trays; leave until set. Makes about 35.

LEFT: *Chocolate Coconut Bars.*
RIGHT: *Lebkuchen.*

Chocolate Chip Cookies

125g butter
½ teaspoon vanilla essence
½ cup (110g) caster sugar
½ cup (100g) firmly packed
  brown sugar
1 egg
1¾ cups (260g) self-raising flour
⅔ cup (130g) Choc Bits
½ cup (60g) chopped walnuts

Beat butter, essence and sugars in small bowl with electric mixer until smooth, add egg, beat until combined. Stir in sifted flour and remaining ingredients. Roll rounded teaspoons of mixture into balls. Place balls about 4cm apart on greased oven trays. Bake in moderate oven about 15 minutes or until browned. Cool on trays.
Makes about 60.

Neenish Biscuits

125g butter
½ teaspoon vanilla essence
¼ cup (40g) icing sugar mixture
1 cup (150g) plain flour
¼ cup (35g) cornflour
2 tablespoons raspberry jam,
  approximately

VANILLA CREAM
¼ teaspoon gelatine
1 tablespoon water
¼ cup (55g) caster sugar
1 tablespoon milk
90g butter
½ teaspoon vanilla essence

ICING
1 cup (160g) icing sugar mixture
½ teaspoon vanilla essence
1 tablespoon milk, approximately
1 tablespoon cocoa
1 teaspoon milk, approximately, extra

Beat butter, essence and sifted sugar in small bowl with electric mixer until smooth. Stir in sifted flours, mix to a soft dough. Knead gently on lightly floured surface until smooth. Roll dough between sheets of baking paper until 3mm thick. Cut into 5cm rounds. Place rounds about 3cm apart on greased oven trays. Bake in moderate oven about 12 minutes or until lightly browned. Cool on trays.

Sandwich biscuits with jam and vanilla cream. Spread a little vanilla icing over half of each biscuit; leave to set. Cover remaining half of biscuit with chocolate icing; leave to set.

Vanilla Cream: Combine gelatine, water, sugar and milk in small pan, whisk over heat until sugar is dissolved; cool. Beat butter and essence in small bowl with electric mixer until light and fluffy. With motor operating, gradually add milk mixture, beat until combined.

Icing: Sift icing sugar into small bowl, stir in essence and enough milk to make a stiff paste; divide into 2 heatproof bowls. Stir sifted cocoa and enough extra milk into 1 bowl to make a stiff paste. Stir both icings over hot water until spreadable.
Makes about 15.

LEFT: Chocolate Chip Cookies.
RIGHT: Neenish Biscuits.

Orange Coconut Biscuits

125g butter
2 teaspoons grated orange rind
1 cup (220g) caster sugar
1 egg
1 cup (90g) coconut
2 cups (300g) self-raising flour
2 tablespoons orange juice
½ cup (85g) mixed peel,
  finely chopped

Beat butter, rind, sugar and egg in medium bowl with electric mixer until smooth. Stir in coconut, sifted flour and juice.

Roll rounded teaspoons of mixture into balls, press 1 side of balls lightly in mixed peel. Place balls, peel side up, about 4cm apart, on greased oven trays. Bake in moderate oven about 15 minutes or until lightly browned. Cool on trays.
Makes about 70.

Lemon Coconut Slice

60g butter
2 tablespoons caster sugar
1 egg, lightly beaten
1 cup (150g) plain flour
2 tablespoons self-raising flour
½ cup (125ml) lemon butter

FILLING
1 egg
⅓ cup (75g) caster sugar
60g soft butter
⅓ cup (30g) coconut
¼ cup (60ml) cream

Beat butter and sugar in small bowl with electric mixer until smooth, add egg, beat until combined. Stir in sifted flours.

Press mixture over base of greased 19cm x 29cm rectangular slice pan, prick lightly with fork. Spread with lemon butter, then filling. Bake in moderate oven about 30 minutes or until lightly browned. Cool in pan. Cut into pieces, dust with sifted icing sugar, if desired.

Filling: Beat egg in small bowl with electric mixer until pale and thick, beat in sugar and butter. Stir in coconut and cream.

LEFT: Orange Coconut Biscuits.
RIGHT: Lemon Coconut Slice.

Coconut Ice Slice

90g butter
½ teaspoons vanilla essence
¼ cup (55g) caster sugar
1 egg yolk
1 cup (150g) plain flour
¼ cup (35g) cornflour
1 tablespoon coconut

FILLING
2 cups (180g) coconut
1 cup (220g) caster sugar
2 eggs, lightly beaten
½ cup (125g) chopped glace cherries

ICING
1 cup (160g) icing sugar mixture
20g soft butter
1 tablespoon milk, approximately

Grease a 19cm x 29cm rectangular slice pan, place strip of baking paper to cover base and extend over 2 opposite sides.

Beat butter, essence, sugar and yolk in small bowl with electric mixer until smooth. Stir in sifted flours; knead on lightly floured surface until smooth.

Press half the dough over base of prepared pan, spread with filling. Roll remaining dough between sheets of baking paper until large enough to cover filling. Lift dough onto filling; trim edges. Bake in moderate oven about 30 minutes or until browned. Cool in pan. Spread slice with icing, sprinkle with coconut.

Filling: Combine all ingredients in medium bowl; mix well.

Icing: Sift icing sugar into small heatproof bowl, stir in butter and enough milk to make a stiff paste; colour if desired. Stir over pan of hot water until spreadable.

Crisp Coconut Biscuits

125g butter
1 cup (220g) caster sugar
2 eggs
2 cups (300g) self-raising flour
1 cup (90g) coconut
¼ cup (55g) caster sugar, extra

Beat butter and sugar in medium bowl with electric mixer until smooth, add eggs, beat until combined. Stir in sifted flour and coconut in 2 batches.

Roll level tablespoons of mixture into balls, press 1 side of balls firmly into extra sugar to flatten, place about 4cm apart on greased oven trays. Bake in moderately hot oven about 12 minutes or until lightly browned. Loosen biscuits while warm. Cool on trays.
Makes about 40.

Coconut Petits Fours

2½ cups (225g) coconut
¾ cup (165g) caster sugar
2 tablespoons self-raising flour
1 egg, lightly beaten
¼ cup (60ml) milk
½ teaspoon vanilla essence

Combine coconut, sugar and sifted flour in medium bowl. Stir in egg, milk and essence. Firmly roll level tablespoons of mixture into balls, place about 2cm apart on greased oven trays. Bake in moderate oven about 25 minutes or until lightly browned. Cool on trays.
Makes about 25.

LEFT: Coconut Ice Slice.
ABOVE RIGHT: Crisp Coconut Biscuits.
RIGHT: Coconut Petits Fours.

Coconut Currant Slice

125g butter
1 teaspoon vanilla essence
¼ cup (55g) caster sugar
1 egg
¾ cup (110g) plain flour
¾ cup (110g) self-raising flour
¼ cup (60ml) milk
½ cup (125ml) raspberry jam
1 cup (150g) currants

TOPPING
60g butter
¼ cup (55g) caster sugar
1 egg, lightly beaten
2 tablespoons self-raising flour
1½ cups (135g) coconut

Beat butter, essence, sugar and egg in small bowl with electric mixer until smooth. Stir in sifted flours and milk. Spread mixture over base of greased 26cm x 32cm Swiss roll pan, spread with jam; sprinkle with currants. Spread with topping to partly cover currants. Bake in moderately hot oven 10 minutes, reduce heat to moderate, bake further 15 minutes or until browned. Cool in pan.

Topping: Beat butter and sugar in small bowl with electric mixer until smooth, add egg, beat until combined. Stir in sifted flour and coconut.

Coconut Macaroons

2 eggs, separated
¾ cup (165g) caster sugar
3 cups (270g) coconut

Beat egg whites in small bowl with electric mixer until soft peaks form. Beat in yolks, 1 at a time. Gradually beat in sugar, beat until dissolved between additions. Stir in coconut. Spoon level tablespoons of mixture about 3cm apart on baking paper covered oven trays; shape into rounds on trays. Bake in moderately slow oven about 20 minutes or until lightly browned. Cool on trays. Makes about 30.

Lemon Coconut Biscuits

90g butter
½ teaspoon vanilla essence
¼ cup (55g) caster sugar
1 cup (150g) plain flour
2 teaspoons water, approximately
1 egg white
2 tablespoons coconut

FILLING
⅓ cup (80ml) water
1 egg yolk
1 tablespoon caster sugar
20g soft butter
3 teaspoons cornflour
1 tablespoon lemon juice

Beat butter, essence and sugar in small bowl with electric mixer until smooth. Stir in sifted flour and enough water to mix to a soft dough. Knead gently on lightly floured surface until smooth; cover, refrigerate 30 minutes.

Roll dough between sheets of baking paper until 3mm thick. Cut into 20 x 5cm rounds, cut 2.5cm centres from rounds. Roll remaining dough between sheets of baking paper until 3mm thick. Cut into 20 x 5cm rounds. Place all rounds about 3cm apart on greased oven trays; brush cut out rounds with egg white, sprinkle with coconut, bake in moderate oven about 10 minutes or until lightly browned. Cool on trays. Sandwich rounds and cut out biscuits together with filling.

Filling: Combine water, egg yolk, sugar and butter in small pan. Stir in blended cornflour and juice, stir over heat until mixture boils and thickens, cover; cool.
Makes 20.

LEFT: Coconut Macaroons.
ABOVE LEFT: Coconut Currant Slice.
RIGHT: Lemon Coconut Biscuits.

Raspberry Coconut Slice

90g butter
½ cup (110g) caster sugar
1 egg
⅓ cup (50g) self-raising flour
⅔ cup (100g) plain flour
½ cup (125ml) raspberry jam

TOPPING
2 eggs, lightly beaten
⅓ cup (75g) caster sugar
2 cups (180g) coconut

Beat butter, sugar and egg in small bowl with electric mixer until combined, stir in sifted flours. Spread mixture over base of greased 19cm x 29cm rectangular slice pan, bake in moderate oven 10 minutes. Spread hot base with jam; then topping. Bake in moderate oven further 30 minutes or until browned. Cool in pan.

Topping: Combine all ingredients in medium bowl; mix well.

Dream Bars

90g butter
⅓ cup (65g) firmly packed
 brown sugar
1 cup (150g) plain flour

TOPPING
2 eggs, lightly beaten
1 teaspoon vanilla essence
½ cup (100g) firmly packed
 brown sugar
1 tablespoon plain flour
½ teaspoon baking powder
1½ cups (135g) coconut
1 cup (250ml) bottled fruit mince

Beat butter and sugar in small bowl with electric mixer until smooth, stir in sifted flour. Press mixture over base of greased 19cm × 29cm rectangular slice pan, bake in moderate oven 10 minutes. Spread hot base with topping, bake in moderate oven further 30 minutes or until firm. Cool in pan. Serve dusted with sifted icing sugar, if desired.

Topping: Beat eggs, essence and sugar in small bowl with electric mixer until thick and creamy. Fold in sifted flour and baking powder; then coconut and fruit mince.

LEFT: Raspberry Coconut Slice.
RIGHT: Dream Bars.

Coffee Nut Crescents

1¼ cups (185g) plain flour
2 tablespoons caster sugar
125g butter, chopped
½ cup (60g) ground walnuts
1 egg yolk
2 teaspoons dry instant coffee
2 teaspoons hot water
½ cup (110g) caster sugar, extra

Sift flour and sugar into medium bowl, rub in butter. Stir in nuts, yolk and combined coffee and water. Roll rounded teaspoons of mixture into 5cm lengths; shape into crescents, place about 2cm apart on greased oven trays. Bake in moderate oven about 12 minutes or until lightly browned and firm. Stand crescents 5 minutes before gently rolling in extra sugar. Cool on wire racks. Makes about 35.

Walnut Coffee Biscuits

1⅔ cups (250g) plain flour
125g butter, chopped
¼ cup (55g) caster sugar
1 egg, lightly beaten
1 teaspoon vanilla essence
⅓ cup (35g) walnuts, approximately

FILLING
60g butter
¼ cup (40g) icing sugar mixture
1 cup (120g) ground walnuts
1 tablespoon milk

COFFEE ICING
1½ cups (240g) icing sugar mixture
1 teaspoon soft butter
3 teaspoons dry instant coffee
1 tablespoon hot water

Sift flour into medium bowl, rub in butter. Stir in sugar, egg and essence, mix to a soft dough. Knead gently on lightly floured surface until smooth. Roll dough between sheets of baking paper until 3mm thick. Cut into 6cm rounds, place about 3cm apart on greased oven trays. Bake in moderate oven about 15 minutes or until lightly browned. Cool on wire racks. Sandwich biscuits with filling, spread with coffee icing, top with nuts.

Filling: Beat butter and icing sugar in a small bowl with an electric mixer until combined. Stir in the remaining ingredients.

Coffee Icing: Sift icing sugar into small heatproof bowl, stir in butter, and enough combined coffee and water to make a stiff paste. Stir over hot water until spreadable.

Makes about 15.

LEFT: Coffee Nut Crescents.
ABOVE: Walnut Coffee Biscuits.

39

Coffee Streusel Slice

125g butter
¼ cup (55g) caster sugar
1 cup (150g) plain flour
¼ cup (35g) self-raising flour

FILLING
400g can sweetened
 condensed milk
30g butter
2 tablespoons golden syrup
3 teaspoons dry instant coffee
⅓ cup (35g) walnuts,
 finely chopped

TOPPING
1 cup (150g) plain flour
2 teaspoons ground cinnamon
⅓ cup (65g) firmly packed
 brown sugar
125g butter, chopped

Beat butter and sugar in small bowl with electric mixer until smooth. Stir in sifted flours. Press mixture over base of greased 26cm × 32cm Swiss roll pan. Bake in moderate oven 15 minutes, spread with filling; cool 10 minutes. Grate topping over filling. Bake in moderate oven further 20 minutes or until lightly browned. Cool in pan.

Filling: Combine milk, butter, golden syrup and coffee in medium, heavy-based pan. Stir over heat until mixture boils, simmer, stirring constantly, about 3 minutes or until mixture thickens. Stir in nuts.

Topping: Sift flour and cinnamon into small bowl, stir in sugar, rub in butter, mix to a soft dough; wrap in foil, freeze about 30 minutes or until firm.

Coffee Hazelnut Biscuits

125g butter
⅓ cup (75g) caster sugar
1 cup (110g) ground hazelnuts
1⅓ cups (200g) plain flour
2 teaspoons water, approximately
2 tablespoons roasted hazelnuts,
 halved, approximately

COFFEE GLACE ICING
1½ cups (240g) icing sugar mixture
1 teaspoon soft butter
1 tablespoon dry instant coffee
1 tablespoon hot water

Beat butter and sugar in small bowl with electric mixer until smooth. Stir in ground nuts, sifted flour and enough water to mix to a firm dough, knead gently on lightly floured surface until smooth. Roll dough between sheets of baking paper until 3mm thick. Cut into 6cm rounds, place about 3cm apart on greased oven trays. Bake in moderate oven about 12 minutes or until lightly browned. Cool on trays. Spread with coffee glace icing, top with halved nuts.

Coffee Glace Icing: Sift icing sugar into small heatproof bowl, stir in butter, and enough combined coffee and hot water to make a stiff paste. Stir over hot water until spreadable. Makes about 35.

ABOVE LEFT: Coffee Hazelnut Biscuits.
RIGHT: Coffee Streusel Slice.

Coffee Biscuits

If Copha is unavailable, substitute 1 tablespoon melted butter.

185g butter
¼ cup (55g) caster sugar
1 teaspoon dry instant coffee
1 teaspoon hot water
½ cup (75g) hazelnuts, toasted, finely chopped
2 cups (300g) plain flour
60g dark chocolate, chopped
20g Copha

COFFEE CREAM
125g butter
1 teaspoon vanilla essence
1 cup (160g) icing sugar mixture
2 teaspoons milk
2 teaspoons dry instant coffee
2 teaspoons hot water

STEP 1
Beat butter and sugar in small bowl with electric mixer until smooth, beat in combined coffee and water. Stir in nuts and sifted flour, mix to a soft dough. Knead gently on lightly floured surface until smooth, cover; refrigerate 30 minutes. Roll dough between sheets of baking paper until 2mm thick. Cut into an equal number of 3.5cm and 5cm rounds.

STEP 2
Place rounds about 3cm apart on greased oven trays. Bake in moderate oven about 15 minutes or until lightly browned. Cool on trays. Spoon coffee cream into piping bag fitted with small fluted tube. Pipe cream around edges and in centres of large biscuits.

STEP 3
Combine chocolate and Copha in small heatproof bowl; stir over hot water until smooth. Dip 1 side of small biscuits into chocolate mixture. Place biscuits chocolate-side up on wire racks; stand until set. Top large biscuits with small chocolate-coated biscuits.

Coffee Cream: Beat butter and essence in small bowl with electric mixer until light and fluffy. Beat in sifted icing sugar, milk and combined cooled coffee and water.
Makes about 35.

Coffee Nut Biscuits

125g butter
½ cup (100g) firmly packed
   brown sugar
1 egg
2 tablespoons dry instant coffee
1 tablespoon hot water
1¼ cups (185g) plain flour
½ cup (75g) self-raising flour
1 cup (100g) pecans,
   approximately
1 tablespoon icing sugar mixture
1 teaspoon dry instant coffee, extra
250g dark chocolate, melted
2 teaspoons vegetable oil

Beat butter, brown sugar and egg in small bowl with electric mixer until smooth. Stir in combined cooled coffee and water, then sifted flours in 2 batches. Mix to a soft dough, knead gently on lightly floured surface until smooth. Roll dough between sheets of baking paper until 5mm thick. Cut into 5cm rounds, place about 4cm apart on greased oven trays, top with nuts. Bake in moderate oven about 12 minutes or until lightly browned. Cool on wire racks.

Dust biscuits with combined sifted icing sugar and extra coffee. Dip half of each biscuit into combined chocolate and oil. Leave to set on wire racks.
Makes about 35.

Crunchy Drops

185g butter
1 teaspoon vanilla essence
¾ cup (165g) caster sugar
2 eggs, lightly beaten
1¾ cups (260g) self-raising flour
¼ teaspoon bicarbonate of soda
2 tablespoons milk
1½ cup (60g) chopped walnuts
¾ cup (120g) chopped dates
¼ cup (60g) chopped
** glace cherries**
5 cups (150g) Corn Flakes,
** approximately**

Beat butter, essence and sugar in small bowl with electric mixer until smooth, add eggs 1 at a time, beating only until combined. Stir in sifted flour and soda, milk, nuts, dates and cherries.

Drop level tablespoons of mixture into Corn Flakes; toss lightly, place about 5cm apart on greased oven trays, flatten slightly. Bake in moderate oven about 15 minutes or until lightly browned. Cool on trays. Makes about 40.

Crisp Biscuits

125g butter
¾ cup (165g) caster sugar
1 egg
¾ cup (110g) self-raising flour
1 cup (90g) rolled oats
½ cup (70g) slivered almonds
1 cup (30g) Corn Flakes

Beat butter, sugar and egg in small bowl with electric mixer until combined. Stir in remaining ingredients; drop level tablespoons of mixture about 4cm apart on greased oven trays. Bake in moderate oven about 15 minutes or until lightly browned. Loosen biscuits; cool on trays.
Makes about 30.

BELOW: Caramel Cornflake Cookies.
LEFT: Crisp Biscuits.
RIGHT: Weekender Biscuits.

Caramel Cornflake Cookies

125g butter, chopped
¼ cup (50g) firmly packed
  brown sugar
¼ cup (55g) caster sugar
¼ cup (35g) self-raising flour
¼ cup (35g) plain flour
½ cup (45g) coconut
3 cups (90g) Corn Flakes
½ cup (75g) unsalted roasted
  peanuts, chopped
1 egg, lightly beaten

Combine butter and sugars in medium pan, stir over heat until butter is melted. Stir in sifted flours and remaining ingredients. Drop rounded teaspoons of mixture, about 3cm apart on greased oven trays; shape into rounds. Bake in moderate oven about 10 minutes or until lightly browned. Loosen cookies; cool on trays.
Makes about 35.

Weekender Biscuits

125g butter
⅓ cup (75g) caster sugar
1 egg, lightly beaten
⅔ cup (110g) sultanas
1 cup (150g) self-raising flour
1½ cups (120g) crushed
  Corn Flakes

Beat butter and sugar in small bowl with electric mixer until smooth, add egg, beat until combined. Stir in sultanas and sifted flour. Roll rounded teaspoons of mixture in Corn Flakes, place about 3cm apart on greased oven trays; flatten slightly. Bake in moderate oven about 20 minutes or until lightly browned. Cool on trays. Makes about 35.

Florentine Slice

185g dark chocolate, melted
¾ cup (120g) sultanas
2 cups (160g) crushed
    Corn Flakes
½ cup (75g) unsalted
    roasted peanuts
¼ cup (60g) chopped
    glace cherries
⅔ cup (160ml) sweetened
    condensed milk

Grease 19cm × 29cm rectangular slice pan, place strip of baking paper to cover base and extend over 2 opposite sides. Spread chocolate over base of prepared pan; refrigerate until set.

Combine remaining ingredients in medium bowl, mix well; press over chocolate in pan. Bake in moderate oven about 15 minutes or until just firm. Cool in pan; refrigerate until set.

Fruity Cornflake Biscuits

5 cups (150g) Corn Flakes,
  crushed coarsely
½ cup (45g) coconut
½ cup (100g) firmly packed
  brown sugar
1 cup (160g) sultanas, chopped
1 cup (170g) dates,
  finely chopped
1 cup (150g) self-raising flour
185g butter, melted
2 eggs, lightly beaten

Combine Corn Flakes, coconut, sugar, sultanas, dates and sifted flour in large bowl, stir in butter and eggs. Roll level tablespoons of mixture into balls, place about 3cm apart on greased oven trays; flatten slightly. Bake in moderate oven about 15 minutes or until lightly browned. Cool on wire racks.
Makes about 35.

Gingernuts

2 cups (300g) plain flour
½ teaspoon bicarbonate of soda
1 teaspoon ground cinnamon
2 teaspoons ground ginger
1 cup (220g) caster sugar
125g butter, chopped
1 egg, lightly beaten
1 teaspoon golden syrup

Sift dry ingredients into medium bowl, stir in sugar, rub in butter. Stir in egg and golden syrup; mix well. Roll rounded teaspoons of mixture into balls; flatten slightly, place about 3cm apart on greased oven trays. Bake in moderately slow oven about 20 minutes or until lightly browned. Cool on trays.
Makes about 45.

Ginger Coconut Slice

60g butter, chopped
1 tablespoon golden syrup
1 cup (150g) self-raising flour
1½ teaspoons ground ginger
½ cup (110g) caster sugar
½ cup (45g) coconut
1 egg, lightly beaten

LEMON ICING
1½ cups (240g) icing sugar mixture
40g soft butter
1 teaspoon grated lemon rind
1 tablespoon lemon juice,
   approximately

Combine butter and golden syrup in medium pan, stir over heat until butter is melted; stand until warm. Stir in sifted dry ingredients, sugar, coconut and egg. Press mixture over base of greased 19cm × 29cm rectangular slice pan. Bake in moderate oven about 30 minutes or until lightly browned and firm. Cool in pan. Spread with lemon icing, leave to set.
Lemon Icing: Sift icing sugar into small heatproof bowl, stir in butter, rind and enough juice, to mix to a stiff paste. Stir over hot water until spreadable.

LEFT: Gingernuts.
RIGHT: Ginger Coconut Slice.

Hazelnut Lemon Slice

1 cup (150g) plain flour
2 tablespoons caster sugar
¾ cup (80g) ground hazelnuts
125g butter, chopped
1 egg yolk
2 teaspoons water, approximately

FILLING
60g butter
1 teaspoon grated lemon rind
½ cup (110g) caster sugar
¼ cup (60ml) lemon juice
2 eggs

Sift flour into medium bowl, stir in sugar and nuts, rub in butter. Stir in yolk and enough water to mix to a soft dough, knead gently on lightly floured surface until smooth. Freeze half the dough for 30 minutes or until firm.

Press remaining dough over base of greased 19cm × 29cm rectangular slice pan. Pour filling over base; grate cold dough over filling. Bake in moderate oven about 30 minutes or until lightly browned. Cool in pan. Cut into squares.

Filling: Beat butter, rind and sugar in small bowl with electric mixer until smooth. Add remaining ingredients, beat until combined (mixture will look curdled at this stage).

Hazelnut Cookies

1¼ cups (185g) plain flour
¾ cup (120g) icing sugar mixture
½ teaspoon ground cinnamon
125g butter, chopped
1¼ cups (135g) ground hazelnuts
1 teaspoon grated lemon rind
1 egg yolk
125g dark chocolate, melted
1 teaspoon vegetable oil

Sift dry ingredients into medium bowl, rub in butter. Stir in nuts, rind and yolk, mix to a firm dough, knead gently on lightly floured surface until smooth. Roll dough between sheets of baking paper until 3mm thick. Cut into 6cm rounds, place about 3cm apart on greased oven trays. Bake in moderate oven about 12 minutes or until lightly browned. Cool on trays. Dip half of each cookie in combined chocolate and oil. Leave to set on wire racks.

Makes about 40.

BELOW: Hazelnut Lemon Slice.
RIGHT: Hazelnut Cookies.

Italian Hazelnut Biscuits

60g butter
¾ cup (165g) caster sugar
2 eggs, lightly beaten
2⅓ cups (350g) self-raising flour
½ cup (75g) roasted
   hazelnuts, chopped
2 tablespoons dried mixed fruit,
   finely chopped
¼ cup finely chopped red and
   green glace cherries

STEP 1
Beat butter and sugar in small bowl with electric mixer until smooth, add eggs, beat until combined; mixture might curdle. Stir in sifted flour, mix to a firm dough, knead gently on lightly floured surface until smooth; refrigerate 30 minutes.

STEP 2
Divide dough in half, roll each half on lightly floured surface to a 20cm × 30cm rectangle. Place half the combined nuts and fruit on edge of long side of dough; roll up from long side. Place rolls, seam side down on greased oven trays. Bake in moderately hot oven about 20 minutes or until lightly browned. Cool 15 minutes.

STEP 3
Trim ends from rolls, cut diagonally into 1cm thick slices. Place biscuits, cut side up, close together, on greased oven trays. Bake in moderately slow oven about 20 minutes or until lightly browned. Cool on trays.
Makes about 35.

Hazelnut Almond Sticks

If Copha is unavailable, substitute 1 tablespoon melted butter.

3 egg whites
¾ cup (165g) caster sugar
1½ cups (165g) ground hazelnuts
1½ cups (185g) ground almonds
¼ cup (35g) plain flour
150g dark chocolate, chopped
30g Copha

Beat egg whites in small bowl with electric mixer until soft peaks form, gradually add sugar, beat until dissolved between additions. Transfer mixture to large bowl; stir in nuts and sifted flour. Spoon mixture into piping bag fitted with a 1.5cm plain tube. Pipe 8cm lengths about 4cm apart on baking paper-covered oven trays. Bake in moderately slow oven about 15 minutes or until dry to touch. Cool on wire racks.

Place chocolate and Copha in small heatproof bowl, stir over hot water until melted. Dip end of sticks partly into chocolate mixture, place on wire racks. Drizzle or pipe more chocolate mixture over plain end of sticks. Leave to set.

Makes about 35.

Hazelnut Squares

250g butter
¼ cup (55g) caster sugar
1¼ cups (185g) plain flour
¼ cup (35g) rice flour
1¼ cups (135g) ground hazelnuts
¼ cup (35g) roasted hazelnuts,
 approximately

Beat butter and sugar in small bowl with electric mixer until smooth. Stir in sifted flours and ground nuts. Press mixture over base of greased 26cm × 32cm Swiss roll pan; mark into 5cm squares. Press a nut in centre of each square. Bake in moderately slow oven about 40 minutes or until lightly browned. Cut into squares where marked; cool in pan.
Makes about 30.

Hazelnut Creams

60g butter
¼ cup (55g) caster sugar
1 egg yolk
¾ cup (110g) plain flour
⅓ cup (50g) roasted hazelnuts,
 approximately

MOCHA CREAM
185g butter
¾ cup (120g) icing sugar mixture
90g dark chocolate, melted
1 tablespoon dry instant coffee
1 teaspoon hot water

Beat butter, sugar and yolk in small bowl with electric mixer until smooth. Stir in sifted flour, mix to a firm dough, cover, refrigerate 30 minutes.

Roll dough between sheets of baking paper until 2mm thick. Cut into 4cm rounds, place about 3cm apart on greased oven trays. Bake in moderate oven about 10 minutes or until lightly browned. Cool on trays. Spoon mocha cream into piping bag fitted with a medium fluted tube. Pipe filling onto biscuits, top with nuts. Refrigerate until firm.
Mocha Cream: Beat butter and sifted icing sugar in small bowl with electric mixer until light and fluffy. Beat in cooled chocolate, then combined coffee and water.
Makes about 40.

ABOVE: Hazelnut Squares.
RIGHT: Hazelnut Creams.

Honey Coconut Biscuits

125g butter
½ cup (110g) caster sugar
1 egg
2 tablespoons coconut
2 tablespoons honey
1½ cups (225g) self-raising flour
1 cup (90g) coconut, extra

Beat butter, sugar and egg in small bowl with electric mixer until smooth. Stir in coconut, honey and sifted flour. Roll rounded teaspoons of mixture into balls, roll in extra coconut, place about 3cm apart on greased oven trays; flatten slightly. Bake in moderate oven about 15 minutes or until lightly browned. Cool on trays.
Makes about 40.

Honey Snaps

60g butter, chopped
¼ cup (60ml) honey
1 tablespoon caster sugar
4 cups (120g) Corn Flakes
⅔ cup (100g) unsalted roasted peanuts

Line 2 × 12 hole deep patty pans with paper patty cases. Combine butter and honey in large pan, stir over heat until butter is melted. Stir in remaining ingredients gently. Spoon mixture into paper cases. Bake in moderate oven about 10 minutes or until lightly browned. Cool in pan.
Makes 24.

BELOW: Honey Coconut Biscuits.
RIGHT: Honey Snaps.

Honey Oat Bars

1 cup (90g) rolled oats
1 cup (160g) sultanas
½ cup (80g) wholemeal
    self-raising flour
½ cup (110g) raw sugar
½ cup (45g) coconut
150g butter, melted
1 tablespoon honey

Combine oats, sultanas, sifted flour, sugar and coconut in a medium bowl. Stir in butter and honey. Press mixture over base of greased 19cm × 29cm rectangular slice pan. Bake in moderate oven about 30 minutes or until lightly browned. Cool in pan.

Honey Lemon Biscuits

60g butter
¼ cup (60ml) honey
1 cup (160g) wholemeal
 self-raising flour
¼ cup (35g) white plain flour
½ teaspoon ground cinnamon
½ teaspoon ground ginger
¼ cup (15g) unprocessed
 wheat bran
1 teaspoon water, approximately

ICING
⅔ cup (110g) icing sugar mixture
1 teaspoon honey
2 teaspoons lemon juice,
 approximately

Beat butter and honey in small bowl with electric mixer until smooth. Stir in sifted dry ingredients, bran and enough water to mix to a soft dough. Knead gently on lightly floured surface until smooth. Roll dough between sheets of baking paper until 3mm thick. Cut dough into 5cm rounds, place about 3cm apart on greased oven trays. Bake in moderate oven about 10 minutes or until lightly browned. Cool on wire racks. Spread biscuits with icing; leave to set on wire racks.

Icing: Sift icing sugar into small heatproof bowl, stir in honey and enough juice to make a stiff paste. Stir over hot water until spreadable. Makes about 30.

Malted Milk Biscuits

125g butter
2 tablespoons caster sugar
⅓ cup (45g) malted milk powder
1¼ cups (185g) self-raising flour
¼ cup (60ml) sweetened
    condensed milk
125g dark chocolate, melted
¾ cup (65g) coconut, toasted

MALT ICING
1½ cups (240g) icing
    sugar mixture
1 teaspoon soft butter
1 tablespoon malted milk powder
2 tablespoons milk,
    approximately

Beat butter and sugar in small bowl with electric mixer until smooth. Stir in milk powder, sifted flour, condensed milk and cooled chocolate. Roll rounded teaspoons of mixture into balls, place about 3cm apart on greased oven trays; flatten slightly. Bake in moderate oven about 12 minutes or until lightly browned. Cool on trays. Spread biscuits with malt icing, then press into coconut before icing is set.

Malt Icing: Sift icing sugar into small heatproof bowl, stir in butter, malted milk powder and enough milk to make a stiff paste. Stir over hot water until spreadable.
Makes about 40.

Malt Biscuits

125g butter
½ cup (110g) caster sugar
1 egg
2 tablespoons golden syrup
2 tablespoons malt extract
2½ cups (375g) plain flour
½ teaspoon bicarbonate of soda
1½ teaspoons cream of tartar

Beat butter, sugar and egg in small bowl with electric mixer until smooth. Stir in golden syrup, malt extract and sifted dry ingredients; mix to a soft dough. Knead dough gently on lightly floured surface until smooth, cover; refrigerate 30 minutes.

Roll dough between sheets of baking paper until 5mm thick. Cut into 5cm rounds, place about 3cm apart on greased oven trays. Bake in slow oven about 20 minutes or until lightly browned. Cool on trays. Makes about 45.

BELOW: Malted Milk Biscuits.
RIGHT: Malt Biscuits.

Raw Sugar Meringues

¾ cup (165g) raw sugar
¼ cup (60ml) water
1 egg white
1 teaspoon white vinegar
2 teaspoons cornflour

Combine sugar and water in small pan, stir over medium heat, without boiling, until sugar is dissolved. Do not evaporate liquid during this process. Bring to boil; remove from heat. Beat egg white in small bowl with electric mixer until stiff peaks form. With motor operating, add vinegar and cornflour, then gradually pour hot syrup into egg white in thin stream. Beat mixture about 5 minutes or until it holds its shape.

Spoon meringue mixture into piping bag fitted with a large fluted tube. Pipe 4cm stars of meringue about 3cm apart on baking paper-covered oven trays. Bake in very slow oven about 1 hour or until meringues are dry to touch. Turn oven off, leave meringues to cool in oven with door ajar.
Makes about 30.

BELOW: Raw Sugar Meringues.
RIGHT: Meringues.

Meringues

2 egg whites
1 teaspoon lemon juice
⅔ cup (150g) caster sugar
150g dark chocolate, melted
1½ teaspoons vegetable oil

Beat egg whites, juice and sugar in small bowl with electric mixer, on medium speed, 10 to 15 minutes or until sugar is dissolved and mixture holds its shape. Spoon mixture into piping bag fitted with a medium fluted tube. Pipe 5cm circles of meringue, about 4cm apart, on baking paper-covered oven trays. Bake in very slow oven about 1 hour or until meringues are dry and crisp. Cool on trays. Dip bases of meringues in combined chocolate and oil; leave to set on foil-covered trays.
Makes about 12.

Muesli Slice

185g butter, chopped
2 tablespoons golden syrup
½ cup (55g) natural muesli
½ cup (75g) plain flour
¼ cup (20g) rolled oats
¼ cup (20g) coconut
1 cup (150g) chopped
   dried apricots
½ cup (100g) firmly packed
   brown sugar
2 eggs, lightly beaten

Combine butter and golden syrup in medium pan, stir over heat until butter is melted; stand until warm.

Stir remaining ingredients into butter mixture, spread into greased 19cm × 29cm rectangular slice pan. Bake in moderate oven about 30 minutes or until firm and lightly browned. Cool in pan.

Toasted Muesli Squares

125g butter, chopped
¼ cup (60ml) honey
1 teaspoon vanilla essence
1 tablespoon milk
1½ cups (195g) toasted muesli
½ cup (45g) coconut
½ cup (55g) ground hazelnuts
½ cup (60g) chopped walnuts
⅓ cup (55g) chopped raisins
⅓ cup (50g) wholemeal
   plain flour
½ teaspoon ground cinnamon
1 egg, lightly beaten
185g dark chocolate, melted
2 teaspoons vegetable oil

Combine butter, honey, essence and milk in medium pan, stir over heat until butter is melted; stand until warm. Stir in muesli, coconut, nuts, raisins, sifted dry ingredients and egg. Spread mixture into greased 19cm × 29cm rectangular slice pan. Bake in moderate oven about 20 minutes or until lightly browned. Cool in pan. Spread combined chocolate and oil over slice; leave to set.

LEFT: Toasted Muesli Squares.
ABOVE: Muesli Slice.
RIGHT: Muesli Cookies.

Muesli Cookies

185g butter, melted
1 cup (130g) toasted muesli
1 cup (90g) coconut
1 cup (90g) rolled oats
½ cup (75g) self-raising flour
½ cup (110g) raw sugar
¼ cup (35g) sesame seeds
1 tablespoon honey
1 egg, lightly beaten

Combine all ingredients in medium bowl; mix well. Mould level tablespoons of mixture into balls, place about 3cm apart on greased oven trays; flatten slightly. Bake in moderate oven about 15 minutes or until lightly browned. Cool on trays. Makes about 30.

Anzac Biscuits

125g butter, chopped
2 tablespoons golden syrup
½ teaspoon bicarbonate of soda
2 tablespoons boiling water
1 cup (90g) rolled oats
1 cup (150g) plain flour
1 cup (220g) caster sugar
¾ cup (65g) coconut

Combine butter and golden syrup in medium pan, stir over heat until butter is melted. Stir in combined soda and water then remaining ingredients; mix well. Drop rounded teaspoons of mixture about 4cm apart on greased oven trays; flatten slightly. Bake in slow oven about 20 minutes or until lightly browned. Cool on trays.
Makes about 45.

Brandy Snaps

¼ cup (60ml) golden syrup
90g butter, chopped
⅓ cup (65g) firmly packed
 brown sugar
⅓ cup (50g) plain flour
1 teaspoon ground ginger

Combine golden syrup, butter and sugar in small pan, stir over heat until butter is melted; stand until warm. Stir in sifted dry ingredients. Drop rounded teaspoons of mixture about 10cm apart on greased oven trays. Allow 3 per tray for easier handling. Bake in moderate oven about 5 minutes or until lightly browned; cool on tray about 1 minute. Lift brandy snaps from tray using metal spatula, roll snaps immediately around handle of wooden spoon; leave to set. Fill with whipped cream just before serving. Makes about 20.

LEFT: Anzac Biscuits.
RIGHT: Brandy Snaps.

Hundreds & Thousands Biscuits

60g butter
½ teaspoon vanilla essence
⅓ cup (75g) caster sugar
1 egg, lightly beaten
1 teaspoon milk
⅔ cup (100g) self-raising flour
½ cup (75g) plain flour
1 tablespoon milk, extra
2 tablespoons hundreds
 and thousands

Beat butter, essence and sugar in small bowl with electric mixer until smooth, add egg and milk, beat only until combined. Stir in sifted flours, mix to a soft dough, knead gently on lightly floured surface until smooth, cover; refrigerate 30 minutes.

Roll dough between sheets of baking paper until 5mm thick. Cut into 5cm rounds, place about 3cm apart on greased oven trays. Brush rounds with extra milk, sprinkle with hundreds and thousands. Bake in moderate oven about 12 minutes or until firm. Cool on trays.
Makes about 30.

Melting Moments

250g butter
⅓ cup (55g) icing sugar mixture
1½ cups (225g) plain flour
½ cup (75g) cornflour

LEMON CREAM
60g butter
1 teaspoon grated lemon rind
½ cup (80g) icing sugar mixture
3 teaspoons lemon juice

Beat butter and sifted icing sugar in small bowl with electric mixer until smooth. Stir in sifted flours. Spoon mixture into piping bag fitted with a large fluted tube. Pipe 3cm rosettes about 3cm apart on greased oven trays. Bake in moderate oven about 12 minutes or until firm. Cool on wire racks. Sandwich biscuits with lemon cream.
Lemon Cream: Beat butter, rind and sifted icing sugar in small bowl with electric mixer until light and fluffy, beat in juice.
Makes about 20.

LEFT: Hundreds & Thousands Biscuits.
RIGHT: Melting Moments.

Honey Jumbles

Honey Jumbles are best made a day before eating – overnight the colour darkens, flavours from the spices develop, and the texture softens. Don't worry if the icing seems a little patchy on some biscuits; this is caused by the icing absorbing colour from the biscuit.

60g butter, chopped
⅔ cup (160ml) golden syrup
1¾ cups (260g) plain flour
1 teaspoon bicarbonate of soda
1 teaspoon ground ginger
1 teaspoon ground mixed spice
¼ teaspoon ground cloves
1 tablespoon milk

ICING
1 egg white, lightly beaten
1½ cups (240g) icing
    sugar mixture
2 teaspoons plain flour
2 teaspoons lemon juice,
    approximately

STEP 3
Roll quarter of the mixture on lightly floured surface into a 1.5cm sausage. Cut into 6cm logs. Repeat with remaining mixture. Place logs about 3cm apart on greased oven trays; gently round blunt ends of logs with fingers. Bake in moderate oven about 10 minutes or until just firm. Cool on trays. Spread jumbles with icing, leave to set on wire racks.

STEP 4
Icing: Place egg white in small bowl, stir in half the sifted icing sugar. Add remaining sifted icing sugar, flour and enough juice to make a thick spreadable icing. Tint half the icing with food colouring, if desired.
Makes about 40.

STEP 1
Combine butter and golden syrup in medium pan, stir over heat until butter is melted, bring to boil, remove from heat; stand 10 minutes. Stir in sifted dry ingredients and milk, cover; stand 2 hours.

STEP 2
Knead mixture gently on floured surface until it is no longer sticky.

Monte Carlos

185g butter
1 teaspoon vanilla essence
½ cup (100g) firmly packed brown sugar
1 egg
1¼ cups (185g) self-raising flour
¾ cup (110g) plain flour
½ cup (45g) coconut
¼ cup (60ml) raspberry jam, approximately

FILLING
60g butter
½ teaspoon vanilla essence
¾ cup (120g) icing sugar mixture
2 teaspoons milk

Beat butter, essence, sugar and egg in small bowl with electric mixer until smooth. Stir in sifted flours and coconut. Roll rounded teaspoons of mixture into oval shapes, place about 3cm apart on greased oven trays, flatten slightly; roughen with fork. Bake in moderate oven about 12 minutes or until lightly browned. Cool on wire racks. Sandwich biscuits with jam and filling.

Filling: Beat butter, essence and sifted icing sugar in small bowl with electric mixer until light and fluffy, beat in milk.

Makes about 25.

Lemon Cream Biscuits

125g butter
2 teaspoons grated lemon rind
½ cup (80g) icing sugar mixture
1 cup (150g) self-raising flour
½ cup (75g) cornflour
1 egg yolk
2 teaspoons milk

FILLING
60g soft packaged cream cheese
2 tablespoons cottage cheese
½ teaspoon grated lemon rind
2 tablespoons caster sugar
1 egg yolk
2 tablespoons currants

Beat butter, rind and icing sugar in small bowl with electric mixer until smooth. Stir in sifted flours; mix to a firm dough. Knead gently on lightly floured surface until smooth. Roll pastry between sheets of baking paper until 3mm thick. Cut into 6cm rounds, place level teaspoons of filling in centre of each round. Brush edge with a little combined yolk and milk, top with another round, place about 3cm apart on greased oven trays; brush with more yolk mixture. Bake in moderate oven about 12 minutes or until lightly browned. Cool on wire racks. Serve dusted with extra sifted icing sugar, if desired.

Filling: Beat cheeses, rind, sugar and yolk until combined; stir in currants.
Makes about 16.

Lemon Pistachio Slice

1½ cups (225g) plain flour
2 tablespoons caster sugar
90g butter, chopped
2 egg yolks
1 teaspoon vanilla essence
½ cup (75g) chopped pistachios

FILLING
60g butter
1 teaspoon grated lemon rind
½ cup (110g) caster sugar
3 eggs
¼ cup (60ml) lemon juice
1 tablespoon plain flour
½ cup (45g) coconut

LEMON ICING
1½ cups (240g) icing
    sugar mixture
1 teaspoon soft butter
1 tablespoon lemon juice,
    approximately

Sift flour into medium bowl, stir in sugar, rub in butter, add yolks and essence; mix to a firm dough. Press dough over base of greased 19cm × 29cm rectangular slice pan, prick lightly with fork. Bake in moderate oven 15 minutes. Pour filling over hot base, bake in moderate oven further 30 minutes or until filling is set. Stand slice 10 minutes, spread with lemon icing, sprinkle with nuts; cool in pan.

Filling: Beat butter, rind and sugar in small bowl with electric mixer until smooth, add eggs 1 at a time, beat until combined. Mixture will curdle at this stage. Stir in the remaining ingredients.

Lemon Icing: Sift sugar into small heatproof bowl, stir in butter and enough juice to make a stiff paste. Stir over hot water until spreadable.

ABOVE: Lemon Pistachio Slice.
RIGHT: Lemon Cream Biscuits.

Italian Lemon Biscuits

1½ cups (225g) self-raising flour
60g lard, chopped
1½ tablespoons milk
⅓ cup (75g) caster sugar
½ teaspoon vanilla essence
1 egg, lightly beaten

LEMON ICING
¾ cup (120g) icing sugar mixture
½ teaspoon grated lemon rind
2 teaspoons lemon juice,
**   approximately**

Sift flour into medium bowl, rub in lard. Combine milk and sugar in small pan, stir over low heat until sugar is dissolved, add essence; cool 5 minutes. Stir warm milk mixture and egg into flour mixture in bowl; mix to a soft dough, knead gently on lightly floured surface until smooth.

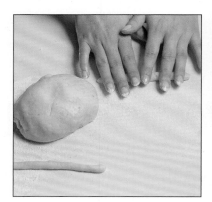

STEP 1
Roll rounded teaspoons of mixture into 13cm sausages.

STEP 2
Twist 2 sausages together, make into circles; press edges together, place about 3cm apart on greased oven trays. Bake in moderate oven about 15 minutes or until lightly browned. Cool 10 minutes on trays.

STEP 3
Dip tops of biscuits into lemon icing; leave to set on wire racks.

Lemon Icing: Sift icing sugar into small heatproof bowl, stir in rind and enough juice to give a soft paste. Stir over hot water until spreadable. Makes about 16.

Viennese Orange Kisses

220g butter
2 tablespoons grated orange rind
½ cup (80g) icing sugar mixture
1 tablespoon cornflour
1 cup (150g) plain flour
½ cup (75g) self-raising flour

ORANGE CREAM
60g butter
1 cup (160g) icing sugar mixture
2 tablespoons orange juice

STEP 1
Beat the butter, rind and sifted icing sugar in a small bowl with electric mixer until smooth. Stir in sifted flours.

STEP 2
Spoon mixture into piping bag fitted with a medium fluted tube. Pipe 3cm stars about 3cm apart on greased oven trays. Bake in moderate oven about 12 minutes or until lightly browned. Cool on wire racks.

STEP 3
Sandwich kisses with orange cream. Dust with extra sifted icing sugar, if desired.
Orange Cream: Beat butter and sifted sugar in small bowl with electric mixer until smooth; beat in juice.
Makes about 25.

Passionfruit Cream Biscuits

You will need about 3 passionfruit for this recipe.

125g butter
1 teaspoon grated lemon rind
⅓ cup (75g) caster sugar
2 tablespoons golden syrup
1 cup (150g) self-raising flour
⅔ cup (100g) plain flour
½ teaspoon ground ginger
1½ tablespoons finely chopped glace ginger
2 tablespoons passionfruit pulp, approximately

PASSIONFRUIT CREAM
60g butter
¾ cup (120g) icing sugar mixture
1 tablespoon passionfruit pulp
2 teaspoons brandy

Beat butter, rind, sugar and golden syrup in small bowl with electric mixer until smooth. Stir in sifted dry ingredients, glace ginger and enough pulp to mix to a soft dough. Knead gently on lightly floured surface until smooth. Roll dough between sheets of baking paper until 5mm thick. Cut into 4cm rounds, place about 3cm apart on greased oven trays. Bake in moderate oven about 10 minutes or until lightly browned. Cool on wire racks. Sandwich biscuits with passionfruit cream, dust with sifted icing sugar, if desired.
Passionfruit Cream: Beat butter and sifted sugar in small bowl with electric mixer until light and fluffy. Stir in passionfruit pulp and brandy. Makes about 25.

Passionfruit Biscuits

You will need about 4 passionfruit for this recipe.

185g butter
1 teaspoon grated lemon rind
¾ cup (120g) icing sugar mixture
¼ cup (60ml) passionfruit pulp
¾ cup (110g) cornflour
1¼ cups (185g) self-raising flour

ICING
1 cup (160g) icing sugar mixture
2 teaspoons soft butter
1 tablespoon passionfruit pulp, approximately

Beat butter, rind and sifted icing sugar in small bowl with electric mixer until smooth. Stir in pulp and sifted flours. Spoon mixture into piping bag fitted with a medium fluted tube. Pipe 2cm × 5cm shapes about 3cm apart on greased oven trays. Bake in moderately hot oven about 10 minutes or until lightly browned. Cool on trays. Dip half of each biscuit into icing, leave to set on wire racks.
Icing: Sift sugar into small heatproof bowl, stir in butter and enough pulp to give a firm paste. Stir over hot water until spreadable.
Makes about 50.

RIGHT: Passionfruit Biscuits.
FAR RIGHT: Passionfruit Cream Biscuits.

Crunchy Peanut Cookies

- ¾ cup (110g) self-raising flour
- ¼ teaspoon bicarbonate of soda
- ½ teaspoon ground cinnamon
- ¾ cup (165g) caster sugar
- ½ cup (45g) rolled oats
- ⅓ cup (30g) coconut
- 1 teaspoon grated lemon rind
- ½ cup (125ml) crunchy peanut butter
- 1 tablespoon golden syrup
- 2 tablespoons water, approximately

Sift flour, soda and cinnamon into medium bowl, stir in sugar, oats, coconut and rind; then peanut butter, golden syrup and enough water to mix to a soft dough. Knead gently on lightly floured surface until smooth, cover; refrigerate 30 minutes. Divide dough in half, roll each half between sheets of baking paper until 5mm thick; cut into 6cm rounds, place about 3cm apart on greased oven trays. Bake in moderate oven about 10 minutes or until lightly browned. Cool on wire racks.
Makes about 25.

Peanut Caramel Squares

- 125g butter
- ½ cup (110g) caster sugar
- 1 egg yolk
- 1 cup (150g) plain flour
- ¼ cup (35g) self-raising flour
- 2 tablespoons custard powder

TOPPING
- ½ cup (100g) firmly packed brown sugar
- 1 tablespoon golden syrup
- 90g butter, chopped
- 1 cup (150g) unsalted roasted peanuts, chopped

Beat butter, sugar and yolk in small bowl with electric mixer until smooth. Stir in remaining sifted dry ingredients. Press mixture evenly over base of greased 19cm × 29cm rectangular slice pan. Bake in moderate oven about 20 minutes or until lightly browned. Stand base 5 minutes then spread with hot topping. Bake in moderate oven further 5 minutes. Cool in pan.

Topping: Combine sugar, golden syrup and butter in medium pan, stir over heat until butter is melted. Bring to boil, simmer, stirring, about 3 minutes or until mixture darkens and thickens slightly. Stir in nuts.

LEFT: Crunchy Peanut Cookies.
RIGHT: Peanut Caramel Squares.

Peanut Cookies

125g butter
½ cup (100g) firmly packed
  brown sugar
1 egg
1 cup (150g) self-raising flour
½ teaspoon bicarbonate of soda
½ cup (45g) rolled oats
½ cup (45g) coconut
½ cup (75g) unsalted
  roasted peanuts
⅓ cup (25g) crushed
  Corn Flakes
⅓ cup (25g) crushed
  Corn Flakes, extra

Beat butter, sugar and egg in small bowl with electric mixer until smooth. Stir in sifted flour and soda, oats, coconut, peanuts and Corn Flakes; mix well. Roll rounded teaspoons of mixture into balls, place about 3cm apart on greased oven trays; flatten slightly; sprinkle with extra Corn Flakes. Bake in moderate oven about 10 minutes or until lightly browned. Cool on trays.
Makes about 50.

Peanut Butter Crinkles

125g butter
½ teaspoon vanilla essence
½ teaspoon grated lemon rind
⅓ cup (75g) caster sugar
⅓ cup (65g) firmly packed brown sugar
⅓ cup (80ml) crunchy peanut butter
1¼ cups (185g) plain flour
1 teaspoon bicarbonate of soda

Beat butter, essence, rind, sugars and peanut butter in small bowl with electric mixer until smooth. Stir in sifted remaining ingredients. Roll rounded teaspoons of mixture into balls, place about 4cm apart on greased oven trays, flatten with fork in a criss-cross pattern. Bake in moderate oven about 15 minutes or until lightly browned. Cool on trays. Makes about 40.

LEFT: Peanut Cookies.
ABOVE: Peanut Butter Crinkles.

Pecan Slice

¾ cup (110g) plain flour
¼ cup (35g) self-raising flour
90g butter, chopped
1 egg, lightly beaten
2 cups (200g) pecans

TOPPING
60g butter, melted
⅓ cup (80ml) golden syrup
¼ cup (50g) firmly packed
   brown sugar
1 egg, lightly beaten
2 tablespoons self-raising flour

Sift flours into medium bowl, rub in butter; stir in egg. Press mixture over base of greased 19cm × 29cm rectangular slice pan. Bake in moderate oven 15 minutes, sprinkle evenly with nuts, pour over topping. Bake in moderate oven further 15 minutes or until topping is just set. Cool in pan.

Topping: Combine all ingredients in small bowl; mix well.

Pecan Biscuits

60g butter
1 teaspoon vanilla essence
¼ cup (40g) icing sugar mixture
½ cup (75g) plain flour
⅓ cup (35g) pecans, finely
   chopped
¾ cup (75g) pecans,
   approximately, extra

Beat butter, essence and sifted icing sugar in small bowl with electric mixer until smooth. Stir in sifted flour and chopped nuts. Roll level teaspoons of mixture into balls, place about 3cm apart on greased oven trays, top with extra nuts. Bake in moderate oven about 15 minutes or until lightly browned. Cool on trays. Dust biscuits with extra sifted icing sugar, if desired.
Makes about 30.

BELOW: Pecan Slice.
RIGHT: Pecan Biscuits.

Shortbread

Rice flour or ground rice can be used in shortbread recipes. Rice flour gives a finer texture than the ground rice.

2 tablespoons rice flour
⅓ cup (55g) icing sugar mixture
2 cups (300g) plain flour
250g butter, chopped

Sift dry ingredients into medium bowl, rub in butter. Press ingredients together to form a soft dough. (Or process all ingredients until mixture just comes together.) Knead dough gently on lightly floured surface until smooth.

Shortbreads can be cooked in many different ways.

• Press mixture evenly into greased 19cm × 29cm rectangular slice pan; mark into squares or rectangles, prick lightly with a fork. Bake in moderately slow oven about 35 minutes or until firm. Cut shortbread where marked; stand 10 minutes before turning onto wire rack to cool.

• Divide mixture between 2 × 17cm round sandwich pans, press into pans; mark into wedges, prick lightly with fork. Bake in moderately slow oven about 35 minutes or until firm. Cut shortbread where marked; stand 10 minutes before turning onto wire racks to cool.

• Shape mixture into 2 × 18cm rounds on greased oven trays; mark into wedges, prick lightly with fork. Pinch edges decoratively with floured fingers. Bake in moderately slow oven about 35 minutes or until firm. Cut shortbread where marked; stand 10 minutes before turning onto wire racks to cool.

• Rub cornflour into design of 11cm wooden shortbread mould; shake out excess cornflour. Press about a sixth of the mixture into prepared mould. Cut away excess dough, tap mould on base to release dough onto greased oven tray. Repeat with remaining dough. Bake in moderately slow oven about 25 minutes or until firm. Stand shortbread 5 minutes before lifting onto wire racks to cool.

Butter Shortbreads

250g butter
2 teaspoons grated lemon rind
½ cup (80g) icing sugar mixture
1½ cups (225g) plain flour

Beat butter and rind in medium bowl with electric mixer until smooth, add sifted dry ingredients, beat on medium speed 10 minutes. Spoon mixture into piping bag fitted with a medium fluted tube. Pipe 4cm stars, about 3cm apart on greased oven trays. Bake in moderate oven about 12 minutes or until lightly browned. Cool on trays.
Makes about 60.

Mocha Shortbread Sticks

250g butter
⅓ cup (55g) icing sugar mixture
1 cup (150g) plain flour
1 cup (150g) cornflour
2 teaspoons dry instant coffee
2 teaspoons hot water
1 tablespoon cocoa
2 teaspoons hot water, extra

COFFEE FILLING
1½ teaspoons dry instant coffee
3 teaspoons hot milk
40g butter
¾ cup (120g) icing sugar mixture

Beat butter and sifted icing sugar medium bowl with electric mixer until smooth, stir in sifted flours. Divide mixture in half; stir combined coffee and water into half, and blended sifted cocoa and extra water into remaining half.

Spoon coffee mixture carefully into 1 side of the piping bag fitted with medium fluted tube. Spoon cocoa mixture into the other side of piping bag. Pipe 5cm lengths of mixture, about 3cm apart, on greased oven trays. Bake in moderate oven about 12 minutes or until firm. Cool on wire racks. Sandwich biscuits with coffee filling. Serve dusted with extra sifted icing sugar, if desired.
Coffee Filling: Dissolve coffee in milk, cool. Beat butter, coffee mixture and sifted sugar in small bowl with electric mixer until pale in colour.
Makes about 40.

LEFT: Butter Shortbreads.
RIGHT: Mocha Shortbread Sticks.

Wholemeal Shortbread

250g butter
½ cup (110g) caster sugar
1¼ cups (200g) wholemeal plain flour
1¼ cups (185g) white plain flour
½ cup (75g) rice flour
2 tablespoons water

Beat butter and sugar in medium bowl with electric mixer until smooth, add sifted flours and water; beat until combined. Knead dough gently on lightly floured surface until smooth. Roll dough between sheets of baking paper until 1cm thick. Cut into 4cm rounds, place about 2cm apart on greased oven trays, mark in half. Bake in moderately slow oven about 25 minutes or until lightly browned. Cool on trays.
Makes about 45.

Lemon Shortbreads

250g butter
1 teaspoon grated lemon rind
¼ cup (55g) caster sugar
3 teaspoons lemon juice
1½ cups (225g) plain flour

Beat butter, rind and sugar in small bowl with electric mixer until smooth. Stir in juice and sifted flour. Spoon mixture into piping bag fitted with a medium fluted tube. Pipe 4cm swirls about 3cm apart on greased oven trays. Bake in moderate oven about 12 minutes or until firm; stand biscuits 2 minutes before lifting onto wire racks to cool.
Makes about 30.

Scottish Shortbread

250g butter
⅓ cup (75g) caster sugar
¼ cup (35g) rice flour
2¼ cups (335g) plain flour

Beat butter and sugar in small bowl with electric mixer until smooth. Stir in sifted flours, press mixture together to form a firm dough. Knead gently on lightly floured surface until smooth.

Scottish shortbread can be cooked in many ways.

• Press mixture into greased 19cm × 29cm rectangular slice pan; mark as desired, prick with fork. Bake in slow oven 45 minutes. Cut where marked; stand 10 minutes before turning onto wire rack to cool.

• Divide mixture between 2 × 17cm round sandwich pans; press into pans; mark into wedges, prick with fork. Bake in slow oven 45 minutes. Cut where marked; stand 10 minutes before turning onto wire racks to cool.

• Rub cornflour into design of 11cm wooden shortbread mould. Shake out excess cornflour. Press about an eighth of the mixture into prepared mould. Cut away excess dough, tap mould on base to release dough onto greased oven tray. Repeat with remaining dough. Bake in slow oven about 30 minutes or until firm. Stand shortbread 5 minutes before lifting onto wire racks to cool.

Viennese Shortbread Biscuits

250g butter
½ teaspoon vanilla essence
¼ cup (55g) caster sugar
1¾ cups (260g) plain flour
¼ cup (35g) rice flour
300g dark chocolate, melted
3 teaspoons vegetable oil

Beat butter, essence and sugar in small bowl with electric mixer until smooth, add sifted flours; beat only until combined. Spoon mixture into piping bag fitted with a medium fluted tube. Pipe 2cm × 6cm shapes about 3cm apart on greased oven trays. Bake in moderate oven about 15 minutes or until lightly browned. Cool on trays. Dip ends of biscuits in combined chocolate and oil; leave to set on wire racks.
Makes about 35.

Rich Shortbread

250g butter
1 teaspoon vanilla essence
⅓ cup (55g) icing sugar mixture
1 cup (150g) cornflour
¾ cup (110g) plain flour

Beat butter, essence and sifted icing sugar in small bowl with electric mixer until smooth, add sifted flours; beat until combined. Spoon mixture into piping bag fitted with a medium fluted tube. Pipe 2cm × 6cm shapes about 3cm apart on greased oven trays. Bake in moderate oven about 15 minutes or until lightly browned; cool on wire racks.
Makes about 25.

Melt 'n' Mix Shortbread

250g butter, melted
½ teaspoon vanilla essence
¼ cup (55g) caster sugar
⅓ cup (55g) icing sugar mixture
⅓ cup (50g) cornflour
2⅓ cups (350g) plain flour

Beat cooled butter, essence, sugars and cornflour in small bowl with electric mixer until thick. Stir in sifted flour. Press mixture over base of greased 19cm × 29cm rectangular slice pan, smooth with spatula, mark into squares or rectangles, prick lightly with fork. Bake in moderate oven about 25 minutes or until firm. Cut shortbread where marked; cool in pan.

ABOVE: Rich Shortbread.
RIGHT: Melt 'n' Mix Shortbread.

Sour Cream Cookies

Beat butter, essence, sugar and yolk in small bowl with electric mixer until smooth. Stir in sifted dry ingredients and cream. Roll rounded teaspoons of mixture into balls, place about 3cm apart on greased oven trays, flatten with fork. Bake in hot oven about 8 minutes or until lightly browned. Cool on wire racks. Dip tops of biscuits into citrus icing; leave to set on wire racks.

Citrus Icing: Sift icing sugar into small heatproof bowl. Stir in rind, lemon juice and enough orange juice to make a stiff paste. Stir over hot water until spreadable.

Makes about 25.

60g butter
½ teaspoon vanilla essence
¼ cup (55g) caster sugar
1 egg yolk
1 cup (150g) self-raising flour
¼ teaspoon bicarbonate of soda
¼ teaspoon ground nutmeg
2 tablespoons sour cream

CITRUS ICING
1 cup (160g) icing sugar mixture
½ teaspoon grated orange rind
1 tablespoon lemon juice
2 teaspoons orange juice,
  approximately

Sultana Biscuits

60g butter
2 teaspoons grated lemon rind
1 cup (220g) caster sugar
1 egg, lightly beaten
1⅓ cups (200g) plain flour
½ teaspoon bicarbonate of soda
½ cup (125ml) sour cream
½ cup (80g) sultanas
1 cup (90g) coconut

Beat butter, rind and sugar in small bowl with electric mixer until smooth, add egg, beat until combined. Stir in sifted flour and soda, sour cream and sultanas. Toss rounded teaspoons of mixture into coconut; roll into balls, place about 3cm apart on greased oven trays; flatten slightly. Bake in moderate oven about 15 minutes or until lightly browned; cool on trays.
Makes about 35.

ABOVE: Sour Cream Cookies.
RIGHT: Sultana Biscuits.

White Christmas

1 cup (35g) Rice Bubbles
1 cup (100g) full cream milk powder
1 cup (90g) coconut
1 cup (160g) icing sugar mixture
¼ cup (60g) chopped glace cherries
1 glace pineapple ring, chopped
2 glace apricots, chopped
¼ cup (40g) sultanas
250g Copha, melted

Grease 19cm × 29cm rectangular slice pan, place strip of baking paper to cover base and extend over 2 opposite sides. Combine Rice Bubbles, milk powder, coconut, sifted icing sugar, glace fruits and sultanas in large bowl, stir in cooled Copha; mix well. Press mixture firmly into prepared pan, cover; refrigerate until set.

Lemon Coconut Squares

250g packet milk arrowroot biscuits
½ cup (125ml) sweetened
 condensed milk
125g butter, chopped
1 teaspoon grated lemon rind
1 cup (90g) coconut
2 tablespoons coconut, extra

LEMON ICING
1¾ cups (280g) icing sugar mixture
1 teaspoon soft butter
1 tablespoon lemon juice,
 approximately

Blend or process biscuits until finely crushed. Combine milk and butter in medium pan, stir over heat until butter is melted; stand until warm. Stir in biscuit crumbs, rind and coconut; mix well. Press mixture evenly over base of greased 19cm × 29cm rectangular slice pan; refrigerate 1 hour. Spread slice with lemon icing, sprinkle with extra coconut.

Lemon Icing: Sift icing sugar into small heatproof bowl, stir in butter and enough juice to make a stiff paste. Stir over hot water until spreadable.

LEFT: White Christmas.
RIGHT: Lemon Coconut Squares.

White Christmas Cups

1 cup (35g) Rice Bubbles
1 cup (100g) full cream milk powder
1 cup (90g) coconut
1 cup (160g) icing sugar mixture
½ cup (125g) chopped red and
   green glace cherries
½ cup (100g) chopped glace ginger
250g Copha, melted
100g white chocolate, melted

Combine Rice Bubbles, milk powder, coconut, sifted icing sugar, cherries and ginger in large bowl, stir in cooled Copha; mix well. Spoon mixture into 20 paper patty cases; refrigerate until set. Drizzle with chocolate; refrigerate until set.
Makes 20.

Chocolate Crackles

4 cups (140g) **Rice Bubbles**
1 cup (90g) **coconut**
1 cup (160g) **sultanas**
½ cup (50g) **cocoa**
1½ cups (240g) **icing sugar mixture**
250g **Copha, melted**

Combine Rice Bubbles, coconut, sultanas and sifted cocoa and icing sugar in large bowl. Stir in cooled Copha; mix well. Spoon mixture into 36 paper patty cases; refrigerate until set.
Makes 36.

Italian Walnut Biscuits

1½ cups (240g) blanched almonds
1 egg white
½ cup (110g) caster sugar
2 tablespoons dark rum
¾ cup (110g) plain flour
1 egg white, lightly beaten, extra
⅔ cup (70g) walnuts,
  finely chopped

Blend or process almonds until finely chopped, add egg white, sugar and rum; process until combined. Transfer mixture to medium bowl, add sifted flour, mix to a soft dough. Knead gently on lightly floured surface until smooth. Roll dough between sheets of baking paper until 5mm thick. Cut dough into 4cm rounds, place about 3cm apart on greased oven trays; brush with extra egg white; sprinkle with walnuts. Bake in hot oven about 10 minutes or until lightly browned; cool on wire racks.
Makes about 35.

Caramel Walnut Slice

½ cup (75g) self-raising flour
¼ cup (55g) caster sugar
½ cup (45g) coconut
60g butter, melted

TOPPING
2 eggs, lightly beaten
½ teaspoon vanilla essence
1 cup (90g) coconut
¾ cup (90g) chopped walnuts
1½ cups (300g) firmly packed
    brown sugar
½ teaspoon baking powder

Sift flour into small bowl, stir in remaining ingredients. Press mixture over base of greased 19cm × 29cm rectangular slice pan. Bake in moderate oven 15 minutes. Spread hot base with topping. Bake in moderate oven further 20 minutes or until topping is set; cool in pan.

Topping: Combine all ingredients in medium bowl; mix well.

Apricot Wheatgerm Crunchies

125g butter
½ teaspoon vanilla essence
¾ cup (150g) firmly packed brown sugar
1 egg
½ cup (75g) self-raising flour
¾ cup (75g) wheatgerm
⅓ cup (30g) coconut
⅓ cup (30g) rolled oats
1 cup (150g) chopped dried apricots
1½ cups (45g) Corn Flakes

Beat butter, essence, sugar and egg in small bowl with electric mixer until smooth. Stir in sifted flour and remaining ingredients; mix well. Roll level tablespoons of mixture into balls, place about 3cm apart on greased oven trays; flatten slightly. Bake in moderate oven about 15 minutes or until lightly browned; cool on trays. Makes about 25.

Sugar 'n' Spice Cookies

125g butter
½ teaspoon vanilla essence
⅓ cup (75g) raw sugar
1 egg
2 tablespoons wheatgerm
1 cup (160g) wholemeal plain flour
2 tablespoons wholemeal
  self-raising flour
⅓ cup (75g) raw sugar, extra
1 teaspoon ground cinnamon

Beat butter, essence, sugar and egg in small bowl with electric mixer until smooth. Stir in wheatgerm and sifted flours. Roll rounded teaspoons of mixture into balls; toss in combined extra sugar and cinnamon. Place balls about 3cm apart on greased oven trays; flatten with fork. Bake in moderate oven about 12 minutes or until lightly browned; cool on wire racks.
Makes about 30.

Marshmallow Biscuits

60g butter
1 teaspoon vanilla essence
½ cup (100g) firmly packed brown sugar
1 egg, lightly beaten
1¼ cups (200g) wholemeal plain flour
½ cup (45g) coconut, toasted
½ cup (125ml) apricot jam,
   approximately

MARSHMALLOW
½ cup (110g) caster sugar
3 teaspoons gelatine
½ cup (125ml) water
½ teaspoon vanilla essence

Beat butter, essence and sugar in small bowl with electric mixer until smooth, add egg, beat until combined. Stir in sifted flour, mix to a soft dough, knead gently on lightly floured surface until smooth. Roll dough between sheets of baking paper until 5mm thick; cut into 6cm rounds, place about 3cm apart on greased oven trays. Bake in moderate oven about 12 minutes or until lightly browned. Cool on trays. Pipe marshmallow around edge of biscuits, dip in coconut. Spoon jam into centres of biscuits; refrigerate until marshmallow is firm.

Marshmallow: Combine caster sugar, gelatine and water in small pan, stir over low heat until sugar is dissolved, bring to boil; simmer, without stirring, uncovered, 5 minutes; cool to room temperature. Beat gelatine mixture and essence in small bowl with electric mixer for about 10 minutes or until mixture holds its shape. Spoon mixture into piping bag, fitted with 1cm plain tube.
Makes about 20.

BELOW: Wholemeal Biscuits.
ABOVE: Marshmallow Biscuits.
RIGHT: Oat Biscuits.

Wholemeal Biscuits

125g butter
¼ cup (55g) caster sugar
2 tablespoons honey
1 egg
1 cup (160g) wholemeal plain flour
½ cup (75g) white self-raising flour
½ cup (75g) white plain flour
¼ cup (15g) unprocessed wheat bran
2 tablespoons unprocessed
   wheat bran, extra

Beat butter, sugar, honey and egg in small bowl with electric mixer until smooth. Stir in sifted flours and bran; mix to a firm dough. Knead gently on lightly floured surface until smooth. Roll dough between sheets of baking paper until 3mm thick. Cut dough into 6cm rounds, place about 3cm apart on greased oven trays, sprinkle with extra bran; prick lightly with fork. Bake in moderate oven about 12 minutes or until lightly browned; cool on trays.
Makes about 35.

Oat Biscuits

3 cups (270g) rolled oats
1 cup (160g) wholemeal plain flour
⅓ cup (65g) firmly packed
  brown sugar
60g butter, chopped
¼ cup (60ml) golden syrup
⅓ cup (80ml) milk

Process oats until finely ground. Sift flour into large bowl, stir in oats and sugar; rub in butter. Combine golden syrup and milk in small pan, stir over heat until warm. Stir warm milk mixture into oat mixture, mix to a soft dough; knead gently on lightly floured surface until smooth. Roll dough between sheets of baking paper until 3mm thick; cut into 6cm rounds, place about 2cm apart on greased oven trays; prick lightly with fork. Bake in moderate oven about 12 minutes or until lightly browned; cool on trays. Makes about 35.

Il Biscotto Delizioso *(The Delicious Biscuit)*

These fragile biscuits must be assembled just before serving.

2 tablespoons caster sugar
2 tablespoons plain flour
1 egg yolk
½ cup (125ml) milk
60g butter
1 teaspoon vanilla essence
¼ cup (40g) icing sugar mixture

BISCUIT DOUGH
1 cup (150g) plain flour
¾ cup (90g) packaged ground almonds
90g butter, chopped
1 egg yolk
1 teaspoon vanilla essence

PRALINE
¼ cup (35g) slivered almonds
¼ cup (55g) caster sugar
¼ cup (60ml) water

STEP 1
Combine caster sugar and flour in small pan, stir in combined yolk and milk; whisk until smooth. Stir over heat until mixture boils and thickens, simmer, stirring, 1 minute. Cover surface of custard mixture with plastic wrap; cool.

STEP 2
Biscuit Dough: Sift flour into medium bowl, add almonds, rub in butter. Add yolk and essence; mix to a firm dough. Knead gently on lightly floured surface until smooth, cover; refrigerate 30 minutes.

STEP 3
Praline: Place nuts on greased oven tray. Combine sugar and water in small pan, stir over heat, without boiling, until sugar is dissolved. Bring to boil, simmer, uncovered, without stirring, until golden brown. Pour sugar mixture over nuts; leave until set. Break praline into pieces, process until finely crushed.

STEP 4
Roll biscuit dough between sheets of baking paper until 3mm thick; cut into 6cm rounds, place about 3cm apart on greased oven trays. Bake in moderate oven about 12 minutes or until lightly browned; cool on trays.

STEP 5
To complete custard filling: Beat butter and essence in small bowl with electric mixer until as white as possible; beat in sifted icing sugar. Beat in spoonfuls of custard mixture; beat until smooth.

STEP 6
To assemble biscuits: Sandwich with filling. Spread a little filling around edges of joined biscuits, roll edges in praline mixture. Dust with a little extra sifted icing sugar, if desired.
Makes about 15.

Walnut Fruit Bread

3 egg whites
½ cup (110g) caster sugar
1 cup (150g) plain flour
1¼ cups (125g) walnuts
⅓ cup (65g) chopped glace ginger
**½ cup (125g) chopped red and
    green glace cherries**
⅓ cup (75g) chopped glace pineapple

Beat egg whites in small bowl with electric mixer until soft peaks form, gradually add sugar, beat until dissolved. Transfer mixture to large bowl, stir in sifted flour, nuts and glace fruit. Spread mixture into greased 8cm × 26cm bar pan. Bake in moderate oven about 45 minutes or until firm; cool on wire rack. Wrap loaf in foil; stand overnight.

Slice bread thinly with a serrated knife, place in single layer on baking paper-covered oven trays. Bake in slow oven about 25 minutes or until crisp; cool on trays.
Makes about 40.

Hazelnut Cherry Truffles

½ cup (105g) glace cherries
2 tablespoons brandy
½ cup (80g) icing sugar mixture
**1¾ cups (190g) packaged
    ground hazelnuts**
1 egg white, lightly beaten
2 teaspoons dark rum
¼ cup (60ml) cream
380g white chocolate, melted
300g dark chocolate, melted
3 teaspoons oil
60g white chocolate, melted, extra

Combine cherries and brandy in bowl; stand 1 hour. Drain cherries, reserve liquid. Combine sifted icing sugar and nuts in medium bowl; stir in egg white, rum, cream, white chocolate and reserved liquid. Refrigerate 1 hour, stir occasionally.

Mould level tablespoons of mixture around cherries, place on foil-covered trays; refrigerate until firm. Dip truffles into combined dark chocolate and oil; refrigerate on trays. Drizzle with extra white chocolate; refrigerate.
Makes about 25.

LEFT: Walnut Fruit Bread.
RIGHT: Hazelnut Cherry Truffles.

Almond Butter Drops

250g packet butternut biscuits
90g butter, chopped
¼ cup (60ml) golden syrup
1¼ cups (100g) flaked
    almonds, toasted
¼ cup (20g) coconut
⅓ cup (65g) chopped glace ginger
100g dark chocolate, melted
1 teaspoon vegetable oil
1 tablespoon flaked almonds,
    toasted, extra

Blend or process biscuits until finely crushed. Combine butter and golden syrup in medium pan, stir over heat until butter is melted. Stir in biscuits, nuts, coconut and ginger; mix well; refrigerate about 30 minutes or until firm. Roll level tablespoons of mixture into balls, dip tops in combined chocolate and oil, top with extra nuts; refrigerate until set.
Makes about 25.

Florentines

60g butter
⅓ cup (65g) firmly packed brown sugar
2 tablespoons plain flour
¼ cup (25g) walnuts, finely chopped
¼ cup (20g) flaked almonds,
    finely chopped
1 tablespoon glace cherries,
    finely chopped
2 tablespoons mixed peel,
    finely chopped
200g dark chocolate, melted
2 teaspoons vegetable oil

Beat butter and sugar in small bowl with electric mixer until smooth. Stir in sifted flour, nuts and fruit; mix well. Drop rounded teaspoons of mixture on greased oven trays, flatten to 5cm rounds; allow about 4 per tray. Bake in moderate oven about 6 minutes or until lightly browned. Cool on tray 2 minutes or until firm. Lift florentines from tray, using metal spatula, to cool on wire racks. Spread combined chocolate and oil onto flat side of florentines, use a fork to give wavy effect. Stand florentines, chocolate side up, on wire racks until set.
Makes about 20.

BELOW: Almond Butter Drops.
RIGHT: Florentines.

Chocolate Hazelnut Royals

90g butter
½ teaspoon vanilla essence
¼ cup (55g) caster sugar
2 egg yolks
1½ teaspoons dry instant coffee
1 teaspoon hot water
1½ cups (225g) plain flour

TOPPING
2 egg whites
¾ cup (165g) caster sugar
1 teaspoon vanilla essence
1½ cups (135g) coconut
½ cup (75g) hazelnuts, toasted,
  finely chopped
⅓ cup (80ml) apricot jam,
  approximately
200g dark chocolate, melted
2 teaspoons vegetable oil

STEP 2

Topping: Beat egg whites in small bowl with electric mixer until soft peaks form, gradually add sugar, beating until dissolved between additions. Stir in essence, coconut and nuts; mix well. Spoon mixture into piping bag fitted with a 1cm plain tube. Pipe mixture around edge of rounds on tray. Drop about ½ teaspoon of jam into centres of rounds. Bake in moderate oven 5 minutes, reduce to moderately slow, bake further 12 minutes or until topping is firm. Cool on wire racks.

STEP 3

Dip tops of biscuits into combined chocolate and oil; leave to set on wire racks.
Makes about 30.

STEP 1

Beat butter, essence and sugar in small bowl with electric mixer until smooth, beat in yolks and combined coffee and water. Stir in sifted flour; mix to a firm dough, knead on lightly floured surface until smooth. Roll dough between sheets of baking paper until 3mm thick; cut into 5cm rounds, place about 3cm apart on greased oven trays.

Almond Petits Fours

185g butter
⅓ cup (75g) caster sugar
60g packaged almond paste
2 egg yolks
2 teaspoons dark rum
1¾ cups (260g) plain flour
icing sugar mixture
2 tablespoons strawberry jam,
　approximately
2 tablespoons lemon butter,
　approximately

STEP 1
Beat butter, caster sugar and almond paste in small bowl with electric mixer until smooth, add yolks and rum, beat until combined. Stir in sifted flour.

STEP 2
Spoon mixture into piping bag fitted with medium fluted tube. Pipe rounds into greased bases of 2 × 12 hole shallow patty pans.

STEP 3
Smooth mixture with spatula.

STEP 4
Pipe mixture around edges of bases.

STEP 5
Bake in moderately hot oven about 12 minutes or until lightly browned; cool on wire racks. Dust with sifted icing sugar, spoon jam and lemon butter into centres of petits fours. Makes 24.

Chocolate Caramel Slice

185g dark chocolate, melted
20g butter, melted
22 ice-cream wafers
20g butter, extra
¾ cup (180ml) sweetened
   condensed milk
1½ tablespoons golden syrup
3 teaspoons smooth peanut butter

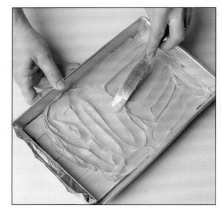

STEP 3
Combine extra butter, condensed milk and golden syrup in medium pan, stir over heat until mixture boils, simmer, uncovered, stirring constantly, about 3 minutes or until golden caramel colour. Stir in peanut butter. Spread hot caramel over wafers, top with remaining wafers; trim to fit.

STEP 4
Spread remaining chocolate over wafers; refrigerate about 30 minutes or until set. Cut into triangles using a serrated knife.

STEP 1
Grease 19cm × 29cm rectangular slice pan, place strip of foil to cover base and extend over 2 opposite sides. Spread half the combined chocolate and butter over base of prepared pan.

STEP 2
Place half the wafers over chocolate, trim to fit; refrigerate 10 minutes.

Chocolate Rum Truffles

185g dark chocolate, melted
½ cup (125ml) sour cream
250g packet plain sweet biscuits
¼ cup (60ml) dark rum
1 cup (150g) unsalted roasted
    peanuts, finely chopped
185g butter, melted
¼ cup (25g) cocoa
1 cup (160g) icing sugar mixture
125g dark chocolate, melted, extra
30g Copha, melted
1 cup (90g) coconut

STEP 1
Combine chocolate and cream in small bowl, cover; refrigerate about 30 minutes or until firm. Roll level teaspoons of mixture into balls, place on foil-covered trays; refrigerate until firm.

STEP 2
Blend or process biscuits until finely crushed. Combine biscuits, rum, peanuts, butter and sifted cocoa and sugar in medium bowl; mix well.

STEP 3
Mould level tablespoons of biscuit mixture around chocolate balls, return to trays; refrigerate about 1 hour or until firm.

STEP 4
Roll balls in combined extra chocolate, Copha and coconut, return to trays; refrigerate until set.
Makes about 30.

Chocolate Brandy Wafers

50g butter
1½ tablespoons golden syrup
2 tablespoons brown sugar
2 tablespoons plain flour
2 tablespoons packaged
 ground almonds
125g dark chocolate, melted
1 teaspoon vegetable oil

CHOCOLATE BRANDY CREAM
⅓ cup (80ml) cream
125g dark chocolate, melted
1 tablespoon brandy
60g butter

STEP 2
Spread tops of half the wafers with combined chocolate and oil. Place wafers, chocolate side up on trays; stand until set.

STEP 3
Place chocolate brandy cream into piping bag fitted with small fluted tube, pipe cream mixture onto plain wafers; top with chocolate coated wafers.

STEP 1
Combine butter, golden syrup and sugar in small pan, stir over heat until butter is melted. Stir in sifted flour and nuts. Place ½ level teaspoons of mixture about 5cm apart on greased oven trays. Bake in moderate oven about 5 minutes or until lightly browned. Remove from oven; cool on tray 1 minute. Lift wafers from trays, using metal spatula; cool on wire racks.

Chocolate Brandy Cream: Place cream in small pan, stir over heat until hot. Remove cream from heat, quickly stir in chocolate, then brandy; refrigerate 10 minutes. Beat butter and chocolate mixture in small bowl with electric mixer until light and fluffy. Makes about 20.

Almond Biscuits

1 egg white
½ teaspoon honey
drop almond essence
1½ cups (185g) packaged ground almonds
¾ cup (165g) caster sugar
¼ cup (40g) icing sugar mixture, approximately
¼ cup (20g) flaked almonds

Beat egg white in small bowl with electric mixer until soft peaks form, add honey and essence, beat until combined. Stir in ground nuts and caster sugar. Roll rounded teaspoons of mixture into balls, roll in sifted icing sugar, place about 3cm apart on greased oven trays, press firmly with fingers to flatten; top with flaked almonds. Bake in moderately slow oven about 12 minutes or until lightly browned; cool on trays.
Makes about 25.

Chocolate Cups

125g dark chocolate, melted
1 egg yolk
⅓ cup (55g) icing sugar mixture
60g butter
125g dark chocolate, melted, extra
1 teaspoon Kahlua or Tia Maria
1 teaspoon dry instant coffee
1 teaspoon hot water

STEP 1
Divide chocolate between 25 small foil cases, spread evenly over sides and bases of cases; refrigerate until set.

STEP 2
Combine yolk and icing sugar in medium heatproof bowl, stir over pan of simmering water until slightly thickened; cool. Beat butter in small bowl with electric mixer until smooth, add egg mixture, cooled extra chocolate, liqueur and combined coffee and water, beat until combined; refrigerate about 30 minutes or until firm.

STEP 3
Spoon mixture into piping bag fitted with a small fluted tube. Pipe filling into chocolate cases; refrigerate 30 minutes. Peel away foil cases before serving.
Makes 25.

Hazelnut Rosettes

250g butter
⅓ cup (75g) caster sugar
½ cup (55g) packaged
 ground hazelnuts
1⅔ cups (250g) plain flour
1 tablespoon Choc Bits,
 approximately

Beat butter and sugar in small bowl with electric mixer until smooth, add nuts, beat until combined. Stir in sifted flour. Spoon mixture into piping bag fitted with large fluted tube. Pipe stars of mixture into small paper patty cases on oven tray; top with Choc Bits. Bake in moderate oven about 20 minutes or until browned; cool in cases.
Makes about 40.

Rum Balls

¼ cup (75g) glace ginger,
  approximately
½ cup (125ml) canned
  reduced cream
½ cup (110g) caster sugar
125g dark chocolate, chopped
½ × 100g packet white
  marshmallows, chopped
1 tablespoon dark rum
100g dark chocolate, melted, extra
2 teaspoons vegetable oil

Chop ginger into 5mm pieces. Combine cream and sugar in medium pan, stir over heat, without boiling, until sugar is dissolved. Bring to boil, simmer, uncovered, stirring constantly, about 4 minutes or until mixture thickens and darkens slightly. Remove from heat, stir in chocolate, marshmallows and rum, stir until smooth. Stand mixture until warm.

Mould rounded teaspoons of warm mixture around pieces of ginger; roll into balls, place on trays; refrigerate until firm. Dip balls into combined extra chocolate and oil, place on baking paper-covered trays; refrigerate until set.
Makes about 20.

Chocolate Chestnuts

60g packaged cream cheese
1½ tablespoons brandy
¾ cup (160ml) chestnut spread
1¾ cups (175g) plain cake crumbs
½ cup (60g) packaged ground
  almonds, toasted
100g dark chocolate, melted
2 teaspoons vegetable oil
2 tablespoons slivered
  almonds, toasted

Beat cream cheese, brandy and chestnut spread in small bowl with electric mixer until smooth. Stir in cake crumbs and ground almonds; refrigerate 1 hour. Roll level tablespoons of mixture into balls, dip into combined chocolate and oil, place on baking paper-covered trays, sprinkle with chopped slivered almonds; refrigerate until set.
Makes about 20.

Italian Almond Biscuits

**2 cups (250g) packaged
  ground almonds**
1¾ cups (280g) icing sugar mixture
2 egg whites
¼ cup glace cherries, quartered
2 teaspoons gelatine
¼ cup (60ml) water
2 teaspoons caster sugar

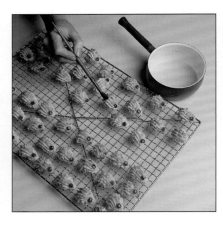

STEP 1
Combine nuts and sifted icing sugar in bowl, stir in egg whites.

STEP 2
Spoon mixture into piping bag fitted with large fluted tube. Pipe 4cm shell shapes about 3cm apart on greased oven trays, top with cherries. Bake in moderate oven about 12 minutes or until lightly browned; cool on wire racks.

STEP 3
Combine gelatine, water and caster sugar in small pan, stir over heat, without boiling, until sugar is dissolved. Bring to boil, simmer, uncovered, 1 minute. Brush biscuits with gelatine mixture; dry on wire racks.
Makes about 30.

Langues de Chat (Cat's Tongues)

These thin, crisp little classic biscuits are good to serve with coffee, or they can be an accompaniment to desserts.

60g butter
½ cup (110g) caster sugar
2 egg whites, lightly beaten
⅓ cup (50g) plain flour

Beat butter and sugar in small bowl with electric mixer until smooth. Stir in egg whites and sifted flour. Spoon mixture into piping bag fitted with 5mm plain tube. Pipe 8cm long strips, (making them slightly wider at each end) on greased oven trays, allow about 6 per tray. Tap tray firmly on bench to spread mixture slightly. Bake in hot oven about 4 minutes or until edges are lightly browned; cool on wire racks.

Makes about 24.

Glossary

ALMOND PASTE: we used packaged, almond-flavoured cake paste or prepared marzipan.

ALMONDS:

Blanched: whole blanched.

Flaked: sliced.

Ground: we used packaged, commercially ground nuts unless otherwise specified.

Slivered: nuts cut lengthways.

BACON RASHERS: bacon slices.

BAKING POWDER (double-acting baking powder): is a raising agent. It is mostly made from cream of tartar and bicarbonate of soda in the proportions of 1 level teaspoon cream of tartar to ½ level teaspoon bicarbonate of soda. This is equivalent to 2 level teaspoons baking powder.

BICARBONATE OF SODA: baking soda.

BISCUITS (cookies):

Butternut cookies: plain biscuits containing oats, coconut, butter, etc.

Milk arrowroot: plain, sweet, fine-textured biscuit.

Sweet: plain unfilled sweet biscuits.

BUTTER: use salted or unsalted (also called sweet) butter; 125g is equal to 1 stick butter.

CHEESE:

Cottage: fresh, white, unripened curd cheese; we used a low-fat variety.

Cream: also known as Philly.

Parmesan: sharp-tasting hard cheese.

Tasty cheddar: matured cheddar; use a hard, good-tasting variety.

CHESTNUT SPREAD: an imported product available from delicatessens and some supermarkets; it is sweetened, flavoured pureed chestnuts.

CHOCOLATE:

Choc Bits (morsels): semi-sweet chocolate chips.

Dark: semi-sweet chocolate; 1 square is equal to 30g.

COCOA: unsweetened cocoa powder.

COCONUT: use desiccated coconut unless otherwise specified.

COPHA: an Australian-made solid white shortening based on coconut oil. Kremelta and Palmin can be substituted.

CORN FLAKES: breakfast cereal.

CORNFLOUR: cornstarch.

COLOURINGS, FOOD: we used concentrated liquid and powdered food colourings.

CREAM (heavy cream): fresh pouring cream; has minimum fat content of 35 per cent.

Reduced: a canned product with 25 per cent fat content.

Sour: a thick, commercially cultured soured cream.

Thickened (whipping cream): has a minimum fat content of 35 per cent, with the addition of a thickener, such as gelatine.

CREAM OF TARTAR: an acid, one of the components of baking powder.

CUSTARD POWDER: also known as vanilla pudding mix.

ESSENCE: extract.

FLOUR:

Rice: flour made from ground rice.

White plain: all-purpose.

White self-raising (self-rising): substitute plain (all-purpose) flour and baking powder in the proportions of 1 cup (150g) plain flour to 2 level teaspoons baking powder. Sift together several times before using.

Wholemeal plain: wholewheat all-purpose flour.

Wholemeal self-raising: wholewheat self-raising flour; add baking powder to all-purpose flour as above to make wholemeal self-raising flour.

FRUIT MINCE: also known as mincemeat.

GELATINE: unflavoured gelatine.

GINGER:

Glace: ginger preserved in sugar.

Ground: ground ginger root.

GLUCOSE SYRUP (liquid glucose): made from wheat starch.

GOLDEN SYRUP: maple syrup, pancake syrup or honey can be substituted.

HAZELNUTS:

Ground: we used packaged, commercially ground nuts.

HUNDREDS AND THOUSANDS: nonpareils.

ICING: frosting.

JAM: a conserve of sugar and fruit.

KAHLUA: coffee-flavoured liqueur.

LARD: fat obtained from melting down and clarifying pork fat.

LEMON BUTTER: also known as lemon curd or lemon cheese.

MALTED MILK POWDER: instant powdered product made from cows' milk, containing extracts of malted barley and other cereals.

MALT EXTRACT: a thick, honey-like concentrate of malt.

MARASCHINO: a cherry-flavoured liqueur.

MARSHMALLOWS: we used packaged round marshmallows.

MILK: full-cream homogenised milk.

MIXED FRUIT: a combination of sultanas, raisins, currants, mixed peel and cherries.

MIXED PEEL: a mixture of crystallised citrus peel; also known as candied peel.

MIXED SPICE: a blend of spices consisting of cinnamon, allspice and nutmeg.

MUESLI: granola.

OVEN TRAY: baking sheet.

PAPER PATTY CASES: cup cake liners.

PEANUT BUTTER: crunchy, also known as chunky; smooth, also known as creamy.

PEANUT SATAY SAUCE: a sauce made from peanuts, onions, coconut cream and spices.

RAISINS: dark seedless raisins.

READY-ROLLED PUFF PASTRY: frozen sheets of puff pastry available from supermarkets.

RICE BUBBLES: Rice Krispies.

RIND: zest.

ROLLED OATS: old-fashioned oats.

RUM, DARK: we prefer to use an underproof rum (not overproof) for a more subtle flavour.

SESAME SEEDS: there are 2 types, black and white; we used the white in this book.

SUGAR: we use coarse granulated table sugar, also known as crystal sugar, unless otherwise specified.

Brown (dark brown): a soft, fine, granulated sugar containing molasses.

Caster: also known as superfine; fine, granulated table sugar.

Icing: also known as confectioners' sugar or powdered sugar.

Pure icing: does not contain ingredients such as cornflour to keep it soft.

Raw: natural brown granulated sugar.

SULTANAS: golden raisins.

SWEETENED CONDENSED MILK: milk with 60 per cent of the water removed, then sweetened with sugar.

SWISS ROLL PAN: jelly-roll pan.

TIA MARIA: coffee-flavoured liqueur.

UNPROCESSED WHEAT BRAN: coarse outer layer of grains removed during milling.

WHEATGERM: small, creamy-coloured flakes milled from the embryo of wheat.

Index

QUICK CONVERSION GUIDE

Wherever you live in the world you can use our recipes with the help of our easy-to-follow conversions for all your cooking needs. These conversions are approximate only. The difference between the exact and approximate conversions of liquid and dry measures amounts to only a teaspoon or two, and will not make any difference to your cooking results.

MEASURING EQUIPMENT

The difference between measuring cups internationally is minimal within 2 or 3 teaspoons' difference. (For the record, 1 Australian metric measuring cup will hold approximately 250ml.) The most accurate way of measuring dry ingredients is to weigh them. When measuring liquids use a clear glass or plastic jug with metric markings.

In this book we use metric measuring cups and spoons approved by *Standards Australia*.

- a graduated set of four cups for measuring dry ingredients; the sizes are marked on the cups.
- a graduated set of four spoons for measuring dry and liquid ingredients; the amounts are marked on the spoons.
- 1 TEASPOON: 5ml.
- 1 TABLESPOON: 20ml.

NOTE: NZ, CANADA, USA AND UK ALL USE 15ml TABLESPOONS.
ALL CUP AND SPOON MEASUREMENTS ARE LEVEL.

DRY MEASURES

METRIC	IMPERIAL
15g	½oz
30g	1oz
60g	2oz
90g	3oz
125g	4oz (¼lb)
155g	5oz
185g	6oz
220g	7oz
250g	8oz (½lb)
280g	9oz
315g	10oz
345g	11oz
375g	12oz (¾lb)
410g	13oz
440g	14oz
470g	15oz
500g	16oz (1lb)
750g	24oz (1½lb)
1kg	32oz (2lb)

LIQUID MEASURES

METRIC	IMPERIAL
30ml	1 fluid oz
60ml	2 fluid oz
100ml	3 fluid oz
125ml	4 fluid oz
150ml	5 fluid oz (¼ pint/1 gill)
190ml	6 fluid oz
250ml	8 fluid oz
300ml	10 fluid oz (½ pint)
500ml	16 fluid oz
600ml	20 fluid oz (1 pint)
1000ml (1 litre)	1¾ pints

WE USED LARGE EGGS WITH AN AVERAGE WEIGHT OF 60g.

USE BUTTER AT ROOM TEMPERATURE FOR BEST RESULTS.

A ROUNDED TEASPOON IS EQUIVALENT TO 2 LEVEL TEASPOONS.

HELPFUL MEASURES

METRIC	IMPERIAL
3mm	⅛in
6mm	¼in
1cm	½in
2cm	¾in
2.5cm	1in
5cm	2in
6cm	2½in
8cm	3in
10cm	4in
13cm	5in
15cm	6in
18cm	7in
20cm	8in
23cm	9in
25cm	10in
28cm	11in
30cm	12in (1ft)

HOW TO MEASURE

When using the graduated metric measuring cups, it is important to shake the dry ingredients loosely into the required cup. Do not tap the cup on the bench, or pack the ingredients into the cup unless otherwise directed. Level top of cup with knife. When using graduate metric measuring spoons, level top of spoon with knife. When measuring liquids in the jug, place jug on flat surface, check for accuracy at eye level.

OVEN TEMPERATURES

These oven temperatures are only a guide; we've given you the lower degree of heat. Always check the manufacturer's manual.

	C° (Celsius)	F° (Fahrenheit)	Gas Mark
Very slow	120	250	1
Slow	150	300	2
Moderately slow	160	325	3
Moderate	180 –190	350 – 375	4
Moderately hot	200 – 210	400 – 425	5
Hot	220 – 230	450 – 475	6
Very hot	240 – 250	500 – 525	7